PERSUASION EQUATIONS

19 Jan 2013

Devon

Let's make it happen,
Roger

Go out and make it a successful day!

ROGER NEUMANN

PERSUASION EQUATIONS

for *instant* sales

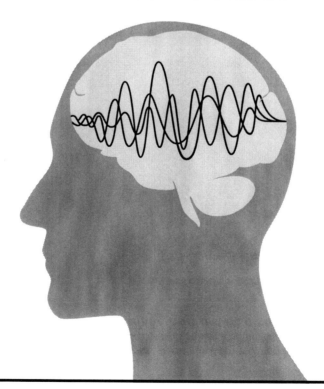

TIPS & TECHNIQUES FOR THE 5-MINUTE CLOSE

Published by Destiny Calling
Cleburne, TX

Copyright © 2011 Roger Neumann

Cover Design and Interior Layout by Imagine! Studios™
www.artsimagine.com

ISBN 13: 978-0-9835326-4-4

LCCN: 2011926830

Second Destiny Calling printing, September 2011

ACKNOWLEDGEMENTS

To write a book like this takes a lot of support and encouragement. I am very blessed to have been surrounded by an extraordinary group of people that inspired, encouraged, prodded and supported me in this endeavor. Naturally, to include everyone that had an input to this accomplishment would be a book in itself; therefore, I would like to thank a few KEY people that helped to make it happen.

The first "Thank You" is to God All Mighty.

Next, I want to thank my Mom, and if she were alive today, she would be happy to see this in print. She was the first person to teach me the art of selling. The strange part about this is she had no idea she was teaching me how to sell.

A special thanks goes to Marshall Sylver, world famous hypnotist, sales trainer, motivation and self-improvement mentor. Without his help, this book would never be written. Many of his words are embedded throughout this book.

The next person is Glen who taught me the skills to become a successful door-to-door canvasser. I am sure he would be happy to see his name here also if he were still alive.

Of course, I have to thank my first real sales trainer, (we didn't have mentors back then) Richard McGinness. Dick, I was always amazed and glazed on the way you handled people and got them happily involved with your product, etc.

A big thanks goes to Jenna Lloyd who was the brains behind getting this information into a book. A special thanks to my sister, Nancy Neumann, and my good friend, Jan McGinness, for your proof reading.

Of course, I want to thank my loving and devoted wife, Diane. Thank you for your positive approach to getting me to write this book and letting me devote my time to complete this venture.

I also want to thank Mike Filsaime for introducing me to Bob (the Teacher) Jenkins. Bob, I want to thank you for challenging everyone in your boot camp last February 2010 to have a book written by your birthday. Here it is!

TABLE OF CONTENTS

Contents

PRELUDE

Twenty-five years ago. On a beautiful late spring evening, two young men graduated from the same university.

These two men were very much alike. Both had been better than average students, both were personable and as young university graduates are, both were filled with ambitious dreams for the future.

Recently, the two young men returned to their university for their twenty-fifth reunion.

These two men were still very much alike. Both were happily married. Both had children. And both had gone to work for the same midwestern company after graduation. Both are still working there.

However, there was a huge difference. One of the men was a manager of a small department of that company and the other was it's president.

What made the difference?

Have you ever wondered, as I have, what makes this kind of difference in people's lives? It isn't the intelligence, talent or dedication. It isn't that one person wants success and the other doesn't.

The difference lies in what each person knows and how he uses that knowledge.

That is why I am writing you about The Wall Street Journal. The entire purpose of the Journal is to give its readers knowledge advantageous for their business.

Recently, The Wall Street Journal made the biggest changes in it's 100 plus years history. The Journal made it easier to access this special knowledge. They added color, made design improvements in every section and today's Journal is NOW more reader-friendly and useful. Today's vital stories stand out to help readers select those that are of interest to you.

It's the best-read front page in America.

Look at page one of the Journal, the best-read front page in America. You see the excellent layout is unchanged; however, it's a faster read. It combines all the important news of the day with in-depth reporting. Every phase of business news is covered such as:

* Business
* Forecasts
* Breaking stories
* Politics
* Stories from Washington, Iraq, China, Afghanistan, etc.

Item after item that could affect you, your job and your future.

If you are short on time, there is a 10-minute scan that will set you up for the day with the latest news.

An improved Wall Street Journal and "the business of life."

Much more than business, the world's most trusted source of business news and information has also added the Personal Journal.

This major new section appears every Tuesday through Thursday. It taps the world's largest staff of business news experts for information of personal benefit to you. Not only personal investing and personal technology, but careers, health and fitness, family and everything about the business of life.

The battle for the consumer.

Marketplace gives you revealing insights into how consumers are thinking and spending and how companies are competing for the market share. In addition, there is coverage of law, media, technology, marketing and the challenges of managing smaller companies.

The best source for news about your money.

Today's Journal is the single best source for news and statistics about your money. In the Money & Investing section, you will find helpful charts that are easier to read and in color. You will also discover three of America's most carefully scrutinized and influential investment columns, which are:

* Abreast of the Market
* Heard on the Street, and
* Your Money Matters.

Every section, feature and column that contributes to making today's Journal the final authority in business news is right there where it's always been and there are two major additions. There is a section called Personal Journal that is about the business of life.

The other section is the Weekend Journal that wraps up the week on Fridays with wise and witty reviews of the arts and entertainment, sports, travel, country life and fulfilling ways to spend your hard-earned free time.

No matter how many times you have looked at the Journal, you should take a close look at today's Journal. It's the talk of the business world. In fact, for business, it is the only newspaper you need.

So what made the difference about those two university classmates mentioned at the beginning of this article? They both graduated from the university together and started in business together. What made their success in business different?

Knowledge.

Knowledge alone is not the answer. They both had the knowledge. We all have heard that knowledge is powerful. That is a true statement when you add another ingredient, action. Therefore, one person took action on his knowledge and the other person did not take action on his knowledge. Knowledge plus action is powerful!!

What type of person are you?

You will discover this book is filled with knowledge. You have to supply the action. Once you do, you can become unstoppable. Read through this book several times and use the gems you will find within the pages. Find and learn how to use one gem at a time. After you have that gem perfected, start with the second gem and build from there. This is a journey and like any journey it starts with one step at a time and continues from there.

The mind is like a parachute. They both only work when they are open; therefore, keep an open mind when your read this book. As you read, keep this in the back of your mind. Whatever the mind can conceive and believe, the body can achieve.

Congratulations on getting this book, I know it will be an asset for you!

DESTINY CALLING!
ARE YOU READY?

What is your destiny? What are your goals? What are your plans to achieve your goals? Whatever the mind can conceive and believe, the body can achieve. You must take action to reach your goals and then you can obtain your destiny.

Destiny, according to Webster's Unabridged Dictionary:

* Something that is to happen or has happened to a particular person or thing; lot or fortune.
* The predetermined, usually inevitable or irresistible, course of events.
* The power or agency that determines the course of events.
* This power personified or represented as a goddess.

You are the power or agency that determines your course of events. Think about that for a while. You control yourself. You make your own decisions. Some are good, some are better and the best are yet to come. To use an analogy, you are similar to fine cheese or a bottle of wine. You get better with age.

You probably purchased this book because you want more out of life. The sad part is most people will never take the first step towards living a fulfilling lifestyle they deserve. You are different and you do deserve a better lifestyle, don't you?

Use your strengths and passion to achieve a better lifestyle by helping other people. The more you give and help, the greater is your return and the closer you are to your destiny.

There are many people who cannot pinpoint their passion and feel like their strengths would not be beneficial to other people. That is a major hurdle to overcome for many people. We have a tendency to do things as second nature or on autopilot. What we do not realize is those things are skills that other people don't have.

There are many questionnaires and tests that we can take to learn what strengths we have and what is our passion. A simple way to learn your strengths is to read the book "Strengths Finder 2.0" by Tom Rath. This book will provide you with a questionnaire that will pinpoint your superpowers.

The sad truth for most of us is that we don't use our full potential. We use less than 5% of our brainpower and we are placed in the category of ordinary. What is the difference between ordinary and extraordinary? The answer is "just a little more."

Do you want to be extraordinary? Are you willing to work harder to achieve more and be rewarded for your extra effort? Working harder means doing steps such as:

* Making one more presentation a day.
* Making one more phone call a day.
* Sending one more email a day.
* Helping one more person a day.
* Writing one more sales letter a day.
* Performing one more survey a day.
* Sponsoring one more person a day.
* Reading 30 minutes more a day.
* Writing 2 more pages for your book everyday.
* Learning new materials everyday.
* Practicing your persuasion 30 minutes more everyday.

* Learning new methods to create more sales everyday.
* Willing to extend your brainpower to work 1% more and be efficient.

Imagine how your life would change if you would do just a little extra. By sowing the seeds of improvement, you will have a bountiful harvest that will change your life forever.

You make your own choices that determine the course of events to obtain your destiny. Start today to make your change. You will learn tips and techniques in this book that will help you succeed. Some of the material may seem strange to you at first; however, they will soon become natural for you.

You will have to practice to become proficient in a relaxed and a non-stressed environment. Remember, you set the tone for the people you are conversing with and if you are calm, they will become calm. Your body language speaks as loudly as your words.

There are many gems within this book and if you use and perfect only one of them, you will realize positive results. Many people will read this book several times and discover something new with each reading. If you will read this book more than once, you too can find another gem you missed on the first reading.

Happy reading.

IMAGINE THE VALUE OF PERFECTING JUST ONE OF THESE STRATEGIES!

Ah yes, another book on how to close the sale. You have read other books on closing sales and have probably picked up a point or two for your sale's toolbox. The books you read were probably written to teach "traditional selling" skills and techniques.

The "traditional selling" methods used terms such as"

* Customer (s)
* Client (s)
* Suspect (s)
* Prospect (s), etc

for the people you wanted to get happily involved with your product or service. Studies have shown that today's people, being more educated, feel like those terms are derogatory. As such, those "old terms" are associated with the "traditional selling" hard pressure closing tactics.

Today's selling does not use that method. Instead, we find the pain or want from the person and we fill that need which takes away the pain. Today, we are their friend and on their side working for them, not against them. We now use a term of "future partner(s)" to replace the "traditional selling" terms.

You have already noticed that "future partners" was used instead of the traditional "customers" or other terms such as "prospects" etc. The mindset of using future partners is to create within the subconscious level a positive emotional feeling of being part of the solution to their issues. The term "customer" gives the subconscious mind the feeling of being used for the benefit of the "salesperson." The intent is to have the benefit go to the "customer" and not the "salesperson." To keep from creating boredom and repetition, whenever you see the words "customers, prospects or clients," think of them as future partners.

There is one element from the traditional selling arena that applies today in our conversational speaking. That element is ENTHUSIASM! There are countless stories of a newbie in sales having more sales and production than some of the old timers in the sales arena. The old timers or pros have more knowledge and skill than the new person; yet, many times the new person outshines the old pro. WHY?

The answer lies with enthusiasm. The new person is so excited that his enthusiasm becomes contagious and his future partners feel there must be something extraordinary with his product or service. After the newbie completes his persuasion, the future partners become happily involved with the product or service. This was done by enthusiasm and the last four letter of enthusiasm explains why? The last four letters are "I A S M" which stands for

I AM SOLD MYSELF

This is the one element that still works today! Believe and Achieve!

Traditional selling worked well years ago; however, times have changed. We are in the 21st century and the sales arena has more sales people trying to sway your prospects to their product or service.

There are more barriers between you and your future partners. That means you need to differentiate yourself from all the others who are selling what you sell. Today you have a smarter, younger, more active prospect who has less time to learn what you have that will help him or her.

If you are going to do well in the sales arena, you must have exceptional persuasion skills. Persuasion is not about a long-winded presentation or not allowing your prospect to speak. Persuasion is about sharing efficient and concise solutions to your future partner's pain.

Mike Morgan says, "Persuasion is helping people decide to do something they would probably do anyway."

You must be able to take your prospects from the position of where they are now and allow them to visualize and grasp the "concept" of your solutions as if they thought of the solutions and claimed those solutions as their own. Once they claim the solutions as their own, the solutions then become real.

Notice the word concept was used above. In traditional selling, we would use canned presentations and responses word for word.

Today's sharing is not word for word; instead, it is concept by concept, discovering the WHY behind every HOW. After you have gotten to the core and discovered the real truth of their pain, you are able to suggest solutions and allow them to heal the pain. This method takes away the memorization in traditional selling and replaces it with personalization.

This book is going to WOW you as you read through the different methods used in the process of closing the sale. You will most likely ask yourself at first if this is a book on sales or is it a book on a completely different area.

As you read, you will pick up jewels and gems that never crossed your mind. You can use your newfound discoveries in your day-to-day living, starting today. After all, aren't we really selling ourselves in our everyday occurrences?

This book is written for the newbie as well as the seasoned pro. Everyone will be able to benefit from the wealth of knowledge, skills and techniques that can be applied and used to enhance their current situation and improve their future.

Keep an open mind and use what you will learn. The question you NOW must ask yourself is; "Am I willing to keep an open mind and learn from this book?" Only you can change you.

Read the entire book. Don't stop part way through the book and say to yourself, "there is nothing new or different about this book." If you feel that way, you have missed the message and process this book provides from the other books you have read.

Many people will read and reread this book and discover something new and different that they had missed the first time through the book. There is a unique twist on the method of "selling" within the book and once you accept and use the unique twist, your results and rewards will be unbelievable. The purpose of this book is for you to propel and excel your sales career. Read the book carefully and listen to what the words are saying.

This book combines two areas into one unique area. The synergy of the two working together in unison and harmony is greater, more powerful, effective and results oriented than the sum of the two working separately.

Knowledge is powerful only when you apply that power and skill to the betterment of mankind. When you perform this way, you will be rewarded handsomely and stand out among your peers.

True, you have read and studied many books and learned sales techniques and closing procedures. You learned the progression of the sale starting from the warm-up period to gain rapport and trust and continually on to the final phase or the "close" of the process. My question for you is this, "how has that been working for you?" Since you have this book, you obviously feel like there is room for improvement. That's great, keep on reading. Don't stop!

There are many people that like titles so let's put a title or label on the type of selling you have been doing in your arena up to this point in time. The title or label for your sales process will be called "traditional selling." It is a process that has been used for decades and has worked for years and years.

As we stated before, your future partners are wiser, more intelligent and obtain more information today than in the past. They also know the selling process as well as you do which means they know when you are about to get into the closing portion of the process.

You probably noticed the words "future partners" were used in place of "customer or prospect." Why would someone use future partners in place of customer or prospect? Subconsciously, people pick up on the words or labels of customers or prospect as a negative. That plays in their subconscious mind as though you are using them as a stepping-stone to reach your destination of success.

Your words are an extension of your thoughts and your thoughts result in action. People will pick up on this so this is your first gem you probably never thought of before.

When you use future partner it gives the person the feeling of you being on his side or his team. People don't care how much you know until they know how much you care. Yes, it is a very small thing to worry about and yet it will have a huge negative impact on the outcome when you use customer, client etc. The only way you can change this is to change your thoughts and words. Let this paragraph sink in for a while. Oh, there's more to come!

Answer this question. What type of business are you in? Are you in the sales business; or, are you in the people business? If you are in the sales business, you definitely need this information. If you are in the people business you said the right answer. This can be explained by the line used by Zig Ziglar, "You can get everything you want when you help people get what they want."

Let your mind go back in time to one of your past sales presentations and in your mind's eye, envision the progress you were making during your presentation. If you had a typical presentation your warm up went perfectly, setting the stage went as planned and all the other key elements worked as you wanted. You did everything as planned and your future partners were in sync with you.

Now, focus on the closing portion of the process, you can NOW remember your future partners becoming more distant, more formal than before, their body language changed from openness to being defensive and their minds were placing barriers and obstacles in front of your offer.

You thought you had a flat drop or a lay down sale and instead you received a NO and not the YES you were expecting. What happened?

That has happened to you, hasn't it? Welcome to the world of traditional sales! Today's customers, your future partners, know exactly what you are doing and the reason you are doing it is for the betterment of yourself. Remember, they feel like you are using them as a stepping-stone for your benefit and not their benefit. At least, that is what they are thinking in their minds. Do you agree it is time for a change to allow you to have better results?

We can break down the stages of traditional selling in the form of a chart. By looking at the chart, you will realize that traditional selling spends too much time in the wrong places.

Traditional Selling

WARM UP	10%			
INFO		20%		
PRESENTATION			30%	
CLOSE				40%

What if there was a better way? What if there was a way your future partners didn't feel they were in a sales presentation? What if there was a way your future partners didn't think of you as a salesman but a sincere solution specialist? That would make a huge difference, wouldn't it?

Before you disregard this concept, think about the times you go to a doctor to "heal your pain." Before you get into the doctor's office, you know you will spend money. You don't want to spend your money and you don't want your pain. After some thought, you realized getting rid of your pain has more value than the value of your money. Said in different words, the doctor's solution outweighs your money.

The doctor spent many years of training, education, in practice and money to obtain his skills to give you the proper solutions to your pain. Therefore, you willing go to his office and give him your money for his solutions to rid your pain. You respect him as a professional and a great asset for your community.

Take a few minutes to study the doctor's story. That is the scenario of going to the doctor's office and paying him for his solutions. Do you call the doctor a salesman? You probably never thought of that and yet he did "sell" you on a solution to your pain. Every time you have a pain you go to him, the salesman, for your solution. Guess what, you are a repeat "customer." Of course, the Doctor has a title on you as "reoccurring patient."

Before the doctor gives you the solution to your pain, what does he do? He will ask how you are feeling and you tell him. If you just give him general information and not a detailed description of your pain, you are not giving him the real reason why you want his help. You are acting like one of your past "customers" who will not give you the specific reason for his wants and needs.

The doctor needs more information before he can give you a solution. He looks at your chart to get your past information and history. He will then ask more questions specific to your pain. He may order some blood or lab work, visually check your body and compile all the information gathered to design and refine a solution to your pain. He needs to be in the information-gathering mode to obtain the right information to prescribe the perfect solution for your pain.

My question for you is this. Why don't you become the doctor in your profession? Obviously, this book will not go into every sales arena and describe the process for that specific area. You are a person that takes action; thinks for yourself and can design your doctor's scenario to fit your specialty.

You need empathy for your future partners' pain so they will open up to you and allow you to gather their information. You can then customize their personal and unique solution to their pain. This book will explain how you can shift from traditional selling to become a sincere solution specialist. Doesn't sincere solution specialist sound much better than salesman?

It isn't your fault. All of your sales training has been traditional selling and your job was to close the sale. What needs to be done is to change your perception. Your perception was enduring your JOB and now it is time for you to start enjoying your career.

The small shift in your mind and thinking will allow you to have happy lifetime partners. A small shift can have huge results. Just a little fine-tuning and attention to details can and will make a big difference for a successful outcome.

An example of that would be a pilot flying from Houston, Texas to Tokyo, Japan. If the pilot takes off from Houston and flies his airplane off course by only one degree in heading of the aircraft, he will be 135 miles off course when he is in Japan. If you are off course in your arena, you also will miss your destination.

You consider yourself a sales pro and you prepare for your presentations. You rehearse your presentation in your mind before you meet your future partners and you have gone over all the possible directions the presentation may go. Every piece of the puzzle was in place and you know the steps involved in the presentation flow chart. You finally get in front of your future partners and start your presentation with the warm up phase and work your way to the closing phase.

During this process you are thinking what do I do next. Guess what, you are working in a logical and systematic format which is controlled by your left-brain. Yes, you are using half of your brain and that half is the one that causes you to highlight **features** of your product or service. You are the perfect blueprint of traditional selling.

Too bad people don't buy on features. Oops, sorry if your bubble is NOW busted. People buy **benefits** or "what will your product do for me?" Your future partners want the feel good or emotional knowledge before they buy. You will sell on emotions and lock in the sale on logic. Sell the sizzle not the steak.

When you get into the emotional aspect of selling, you are using the right side of your brain and your questions are "what do I ask?" Ask, then tell (share), if you want to sell.

The following chart shows the time spent in each phase in the sincere sharing scenario:

Natural Persuasion

GATHER INFO AND BUILD RELATIONSHIP				90%
PRESENTATION	5%			
CLOSE	5%			

By comparing the two charts, you will see there is a huge difference placed on the process of getting your future partners happily involved with your product or service. Once you make the transition from traditional selling to being a sincere solution specialist, you will be amazed and glazed.

You are NOW asking yourself how do I make the transition from one to the other. It takes practice, practice and more practice. You have established your unique process that you feel has been working for you in the past. Didn't that take practice, practice and more practice to get to that level in your career? If there was a way to improve on your skills, you do want to learn and apply them, don't you?

Some advice to help you make the transition is to forget about the past skills and procedures you used with traditional selling. You used a system and you have adopted a preconceived mindset of the way your sales presentation would be given and you knew how you were going to close the sale.

Using today's methods, you will experience answers that you have not expected because they will NOT be the familiar answers you were getting with your traditional selling presentations. Your customers of today do not fit the mode of your customers from yesterday. Do not prejudge people today by the way they dress, look, where they live or what type of work they do. We are not clones.

What worked for you years ago will not work well for you today. If you keep thinking, "I thought" the people would be like they were years ago, you need to work on your situation awareness. Times have changed and people changed. The people of today are much more informed than the people of yesterday. Modern technology has given every person the opportunity to enhance his intelligence and aware- ness. This may seem like a setback for you; however, it is a setup for your new beginning to reach your destiny. Is the new way a good way? Here is your answer! "The glory of this present house will be greater than the glory of the former house." Haggai 2:9

Don't worry; you already know what to do. You just need a realign- ment of your knowledge and skills to perform in a more efficient and effective manner. The realignment will have you:

* Listening better.
* Asking feeling questions.
* Repeating what your future partners just shared with you.
* Structure your solutions to fit the scenario.

Fill in the charts with the proper time spent in each phase.

Traditional Selling

WARM UP				
INFO				
PRESENTATION				
CLOSE				

Natural Persuasion

GATHER INFO AND BUILD RELATIONSHIP				
PRESENTATION				
CLOSE				

The proper time spent in each phase:

Traditional Selling

WARM UP	10%			
INFO		20%		
PRESENTATION			30%	
CLOSE				40%

Natural Persuasion

GATHER INFO AND BUILD RELATIONSHIP				90%
PRESENTATION	5%			
CLOSE	5%			

LISTENING . . . the secret of sales superstars!

Listen and hear what your clients are saying. Too many people just listen to what the other person is saying and don't really hear what is said. You need to listen to every word and not be thinking of what to say after the person quits speaking.

Can you honestly say you listen and hear every word the other person is saying during your presentation? Is your mind a step ahead of the other person so you will be ready to reply with your next set of words that follows in your presentation flowchart or checklist? If you don't listen to every word, how can you respond to their statement with any substance and accuracy?

Your future partners are giving you information about their situation and that information opens the door for you to respond specifically to what they just shared with you what they want and need. Your act of listening without judgment or bias and focusing on them is so unique and powerful that you will attract people as a magnet.

This is where you can shine and be their hero. In addition to that, you have the skill of asking pertinent questions, listening to their answers, and asking more questions from their answers to get a deeper understanding of their wants and needs. You set yourself above the others.

Gathering all the proper information allows you to give them a unique and custom designed solution to fulfill their needs, wants and desires. That is what a sincere solution specialist does for his future partners. As a sincere solution specialist, listening is the greatest personal skill you can ever master. There is a reason why our Master created us with two ears and only one mouth.

Why ask warm fuzzy feeling questions?

Once you have perfected the skill of 100% listening, you are NOW in the proper position to ask the questions of finding their WHY for your product or service. In this process you will ask many questions to find the real reason WHY your prospects want and need your solution to their pain. Think of the process being similar to peeling an onion layer after layer to get to the core of the matter. You will receive answers that are not the real reason or WHY if you try to penetrate into the core too soon. After you have discovered the root of their issue, or their WHY, you have obtained the information needed to custom design a solution that will eliminate their pain.

Using this method, your prospects believe it was their words that allowed you to help them rid their pain and their subconscious brain will take credit for the solution. The new information takes some time for their subconscious mind to absorb then process that information. After the processing, the information is transferred to the conscious mind. If they think "it" is true, then it is true for them.

Too many people want to rush the sales close. Don't do that. This is the place where you should be the most relaxed, non-threatening and say the least amount as possible.

Your future partners are NOW painting pictures in their mind's eyes of the benefits they will have from your solution. They are in a trance painting their beautiful picture into the future. At this point in time, they are selling themselves so don't screw it up by talking.

This trance is called the Alpha stage in the field of hypnosis and we have all been there. This is the stage and time during your information gathering where your future partners are absorbing the information and processing their idea to use your solution to overcome their pain. This does not happen within a few seconds so you must give your future partners time to feel and experience the outcome for their benefit.

When you listen, how much do you hear?

You are listening 100% of the time and you are asking the right questions. Before you ask those questions, always repeat what the person said before you ask your next question. This will ensure what you thought you heard was really what you heard and what the person said.

By using this technique, you will stay on the same wavelength as the other person or another way of saying this is you are on the same track with them. When you repeat what you heard, your future partners also hears from you what they said and if the message was not what they wanted, they will restate their message.

You once again will repeat what they said and they confirm the message as the one they wanted you to hear. You are making progress.

This form of listening makes you smarter because it keeps you on the right track and you don't go off into tangents. This is a synergistic process of listening and asking the proper questions and is greater than the sum of each separately. If you don't listen 100% of the time or as it is called, lazy listening, your communication is weakened and you are apt to ask questions not related to your clients answers.

This is part of the traditional selling process. Don't go there. Remember, your job is not to sell products or services; it is to solve problems by offering a solution.

How would you do it?

As an information seeker, or detective, you discover clues and information on the future partners needs, wants and desires. With that knowledge, you can NOW structure your service to fulfill those needs wants and desires. You are the person that guided your future partners to discovering their solution to their challenges. Yes, you are in the business of helping people. By using these steps, you will become a sincere solution specialist.

Obviously, this is a different road to take than the road of traditional selling. Salespeople, suspects, prospects, customers, clients, business associates, business partners etc have traveled the road of traditional selling for many decades. Since this has been such a heavily traveled road everyone knows where the bumps are, the detours, traffic jams and obstructions are along the route.

When you take a different route, your future partners will get a feeling of freedom and openness because it is not the same old routine. The drive on this route will be much smoother, more enjoyable and less stressful for you and your future partners. Happy motoring!

You do these four steps by communications using your non-verbal and verbal skills. Your verbal communication is accomplished by your words or dialogue. A dialogue is a conversation by two or more people exchanging ideas, thoughts or opinions on a subject and arriving at a common agreement. To accomplish this you use words to arrive at the same conclusion. Words are powerful.

Words alone are not enough to reach your destination; you also need great people skills. You are in a people business and you should know how to treat people the way they want to be treated. Put yourself in the shoes of your future partners and find the solution to their pain. When you are with your future partners you must find the problem, challenge or pain first before you can share your solution to their problem, challenge or pain. Take your time and do not rush this process.

You have just read several pages on a different approach to salesmanship. This is a new approach if you have been in sales for years and you are asking yourself if an old dog can learn new "tricks" and procedures. The short answer is absolutely yes and it all depends on YOU.

At the present time what you have read is theory and until you implement the procedures, it will stay as theory. Are you ready for your realignment? You have all the knowledge you need to succeed if you want to succeed. Here is a simple guide to help you change from salesman to sincere solution specialist.

Practice to become a PRO.

You had to practice when you learned how to sell and you were successful. Nothing beats practice except for more practice. As we go through this book you will learn how to arrange your words, how to pace your speech, how to use your body language and many other factors involved with the process.

Don't let this overwhelm you because you won't learn it in one setting and you will need to repeat items until they become second nature to you. Practice does make perfect. Take it one step at a time.

Quantity verse quality.

In sales and sales calls, we prefer quality calls verses quantity calls. Makes sense doesn't it? I say no, it makes dollars! This is a numbers game with a twist. We are not trying to present to as many people as we can in a day; we are trying to have as many QUALITY solution solving presentations as we can in a day.

It is logical that you would want to be in front of as many targeted future partners as you can in one day. These are the people you want and they will allow you to practice your skills while you help them. If you improve only 20% or 30% from your old style of selling, you will discover a huge increase in your bank account. Think of this as getting paid to learn. EARN WHILE YOU LEARN!

Relax your way to wealth.

Studies have shown that the majority of the sales force gets stressed when they are in a sales presentation. If you fit into that category, you need to sit back, breathe through your nose and smell the roses. If you are tense, your future partners will pick up on that and they will become tense. Now you just created a barrier between you and them. You are in front of them as a friend and someone that is going to help them remove their pain. Remember, you are now the doctor and you know how to make them well. When your future partners know you care about them, they will help you help them.

Don't think about the END, concentrate on the JOURNEY.

You are on a mission to help people and not to close a sale. Use your professional skills in asking the right questions to uncover their needs and wants. Your only purpose at this point is to have a solution that your future partners want and allow them to absorb your solution into their subconscious mind and process that information to their conscious mind. This creates a strong and trusting relationship and you will discover benefits from your process. If you don't concentrate on your outcome, your income will increase.

Pace yourself, don't go for the Jugular Vein.

Patience is golden. There will be times during your discussion with your future partners when they will make a statement that is a golden opportunity to go for the close. Don't do it, that's traditional selling. People will make statements without any creditability behind them.

Example, have you been in a presentation when someone would say "I would like to make more money?" Of course, we all have. If you had a program that would provide them more money and you told them about that program at that time, how did that work for you? Nope, it didn't work well. The reason is the person was just talking to be talking and wasn't really sharing the real issue with you. That's an example of a layer to the onion analogy. You must be sure of the real issue before you can design their solution. Are you aware that premature closing is the main reason for resistance?

Just like making LOVE.

The expression slow and easy describes your game plan. According to the chart on pages 26 and 27, 90% of your time with your future partners is spent gathering information and constructing a solution that will fill their needs and wants. The more quality questions you ask the more your future partners will share with you and in that process your future partners are closing themselves. Think of this as a process or journey without a time limit. Give your people time to sell themselves in their minds.

You just read that telling instead of asking is old school. You also learned the "sale" is not made at the end, it's made throughout the conversational and information gathering process. This is the quality time you spend with your future partners to gain rapport, trust, and respect and become part of a new bonding friendship.

Since you have made that transition from a salesman to a friend, they will open up to you and tell you what they want and the WHY behind the want. At this point in your information gathering, your future partners are comfortable with you. They share their past history, where they are today and what they know they need to change to improve their lives and obtain their wants.

Do you feel this information could assist you in designing a solution to fulfill their wants? You better, because they just sold themselves.

You asked enough questions and learned from their answers that there is a need for them to make a change to eliminate their pain. You've done all of this without using any manipulative sales closes or techniques that cause rejections and you did this in a calm, relaxed and stress free manner. Congratulations, you did it perfectly!

Here is a key point for you to take the next critical step in the process. You do not tell them you know a solution for their wants and needs; instead, you suggest you "may know of a solution" that could take care of their needs and wants.

With that little tidbit of information, your future partners know the value of your solution is priceless and they will ask you to explain your solution. If they have a pain and you have a cure, it goes back to the beginning with the doctor's scenario and you are NOW their doctor.

The only thing left to do is explain their solution, give them "time to process" and realize the benefits, then follow up with completing the paperwork. If you are asking yourself if this can be that easy the answer is YES once you learn the process and skills of controlling the process.

Take some time now and reflect on how you arrived at this position during your presentation. Listening to your future partners' comments and answers did this. Listening is a key element to the process. How good are your listening skills? Take this short survey below and find out.

YOU will learn from this:

- Do you think about other things while you're keeping track of the conversation? Y N
- Do you think about what you are going to say next? Y N
- Do you listen with the intent to reply rather than the intent to understand? Y N
- Do you interrupt with your own ideas before the other person has finished talking? Y N
- Do you primarily listen for facts rather than ideas? Y N
- Do you tune out things you feel will be too difficult to understand? Y N
- Do you try to make it appear you are paying attention when you are not? Y N
- Do certain words or phrases prejudice you so that you don't listen objectively? Y N
- Do your thoughts turn to other things when you believe a speaker will have nothing interesting to say? Y N
- Do you finish other people's sentences? Y N
- Can you tell from a person's appearance and delivery that he won't have anything important to say? Y N
- Are you easily distracted by outside sights and sounds? Y N

By Michael Oliver

How did you do after the quiz? You had at least one "YES," didn't you? Studies have proven "sales people" especially do not listen. Very,

very, very few people answer all No's! If you marked a yes anywhere on the list, you need to work on your listening skills. We were never taught how to listen correctly. The good news is this; good listening habits can be learned.

You do listen, don't you?

When I speak in front of a group of people I like to share a small story with the group. Now is a good time to get a piece of paper and a pen or pencil for taking notes. Just pretend you are listening as you read this:

You are a school bus driver and your job is to pick up the school children and take them to school in the mornings.

You drive your bus out of the schoolyard heading south for 1/4 mile.

You turn right going west for 3/8 of a mile and turn right heading north for 2 miles when you stop and pick up 5 school kids, 3 girls and 2 boys.

You proceed for 1/4 of a mile, turn right going east for 2 & 1/4 miles and pick up 3 boys and 4 girls. You continue east for 1/8 of a mile, turn right heading south for 1/2 of a mile and pick up 6 boys and 2 girls.

You continue on for 1 & 3/4 miles and turn right heading west for 2 miles and you turn right going back into the schoolyard and the school kids disembark the bus.

Now, based on the information you just received, write on the piece of paper the **age of the bus driver**. I'll wait.

You're not writing, why?

You say you need more information.

Most sales people don't really listen.

In less than two minutes, you were told ten times YOU are a bus driver! So my question is this. How old are you?

After the quiz and the short story, how do you feel NOW? Yes, listening is critical and it affects your bottom line one way or another. We can sum up everything in this one statement: Let every person be quick to listen, slow to speak. James 1:19

Right about now you are thinking this makes sense to me and is logical for those who are belly to belly with their future partners. How does this apply to people that market online via the internet? The principles are the same with a few modifications.

When you market online your ads must draw the attention of your visitors to your site. Ads should be informative, intriguing, alluring, action oriented and having your viewers wanting more. Write your title as a micro sales page. We know visitors will decide within seconds if they want to leave your ad or will click to learn more.

Let your visitor know the solution to his pain is just a click away. Use verbs that are action packed and a few bullet points to create the undesirable urge to click and learn more on the following page. Here is an example:

The Sultry, Voluptuous, Sexy Vixen Sucks Her Men Of Prey Into Her Tangled Web Of Degradation And Deceit!

Want to learn her skills?

CLICK HERE

What image is NOW in your mind? Is it a dominatrix wearing black leather, with whips and chains and kicking her prey with her high heel stilettos?

Interest, intrigue and the unknown create curiosity that moves a person to wanting more. When you get your visitors to wanting more and you offer a way for them to get that "more," you have acquired another future partner.

Another secret piece to the puzzle.

Another piece of the puzzle along your journey to a successful sincere solution specialist is to use a subtle form of hypnosis. No, you are not going to become a hypnotist. However, you will learn how to realign and use your words and actions to influence and persuade your future partners' minds.

Words are powerful and when you use them properly you will help people. This really is a win-win situation.

Let's set up a hypothetical scenario. You are in one of the great cities in the U.S. where the weather is picture perfect nearly every day of the year. Let's use the city of San Diego, California and it is one of those perfect, postcard days. The weather is perfect and everyone is in a great mood. Since it is such a perfect day, you decide to go for a drive.

As you are driving, you pass an exotic and classic car lot. In the back of your mind, you have always wanted a classic car. You pull into the lot just to see what types of cars they have available. When you pulled into the lot, you spotted a 1957 red Thunderbird convertible. You park your car and walk to the Thunderbird and your heart begins to beat faster as you get nearer to the Thunderbird. As you stand there, you are saying to yourself, this is the car I have always wanted since I was a teenager. While you are inspecting the Thunderbird, the "salesman" walks to you and he says the following:

Hello!

It's a great day, isn't it? (you) YES

I see you do spot quality right away, don't you? (you) YES

You would look fantastic driving around town in this beauty, wouldn't you? (you) YES

What just happened and what did he just do to you? He used subtle hypnosis and got you saying "YES" three times in a row and he now has your subconscious mind in the positive mindset. We will get into this deeper in the book.

TRUTHS OF THE BUYING MIND

In a moment you will learn methods used for persuasion.

Most of them can be used for inside sales, outside sales and the internet.

Our mind is a powerful and unbelievable instrument. It controls everything we think, do and say. We have a subconscious mind and a conscious mind.

Which of the two controls our buying? Could it be the subconscious mind or could it be the conscious mind?

You probably are now using your conscious mind to decide your answer.

Those of you that said the buying is done by the subconscious mind I want to say congratulations, you are correct.

For those of you that said the buying is done by the conscious mind, I have to say congratulations also because that is correct.

The two minds work in harmony to solidify a buying process.

The subconscious mind is the emotional part of the mind and we do buy on emotions.

The conscious mind is the logical part of our mind and it uses data and facts to lock in the purchase you just made.

That is the reason we need to focus on both minds at the close. Close the sale on emotions and lock it in with logic.

This works on all three types of sales I mentioned. They are inside, outside and internet sales.

Many sales have canceled because the sales person did not lock in the sale with logic and the future partners had buyer's remorse the next day and canceled their purchase.

A true professional will use a form of hypnosis during the persuasion.

It's not the form of hypnosis that has a person barking like a dog or clucking like a chicken. That type of hypnosis is left to the stage professionals.

It's the hypnosis of using tonality, the correct words in the correct order. Using the words with the correct inflection and speed.

Words are powerful when you know how to use them to control, or influence, your future partner's mind.

There will be times when you will have to think outside of the box and be creative with your words. Use your words to plant that seed into the future partner's mind of NOW wanting your product or service.

A professional can give a suggestion to his future partner and have him thinking that suggestion was his idea.

When he thinks the suggestion was his idea, then the suggestion becomes factual. In his mind, he was the one who thought of it and took action on that suggestion.

A word of caution, your future partner cannot become aware of you doing this to him. It must be done very subtly.

"ALL THAT A MAN ACHIEVES AND ALL THAT HE FAILS TO ACHIEVE IS THE DIRECT RESULT OF HIS OWN THOUGHTS."

by James Allen

THESE 3 KEYS WILL UNLOCK YOUR FINANCIAL VAULT

Representational systems is a term used to describe how people express themselves to other people and the world. It is the way everyone thinks and talks about their surroundings, beliefs and everyday activities. There are three main groups within the system. We use all three of the groups when we converse with someone; however, every person has a primary group for conversation and communication. The three groups are:

- visual
- auditory
- kinesics

We know as a solution specialist, we must gain rapport with people in order for them to like and trust us. In fact, from the "NATURAL PERSUASION" chart, we learned that we acquire this during our information gathering and creating a relationship phase. This is a very important phase and it involves 90% of our time when we are talking with people.

We must act like a chameleon and change our colors to fit in with the environment. Said another way, we must use the same representational system our future partners use to establish rapport. If we use the wrong system, it will have the affect of talking a different language than they. If you speak English and they speak Greek, there will not be quality rapport and the way you represent things will not be accepted.

During your rapport period you must determine which of the three systems are dominant for your people. Once you establish the proper system you should converse with them in their preferred system. This will let your future partners realize you are like them and that will enhance their like and trust in you. You are gaining rapport. Many "salespeople" that don't use this method are the ones that don't get their prospects happily involved with their product or service.

The visual system uses the arena of seeing things or painting a picture in your mind's eye. People in this system would rather see information than hear information or having the feelings of something happening.

This group likes to go to movies, watch TV, go to art shows or any thing that involve the visual arena. They like bright colors, they have a great outlook on things, they use maps or a gps for directions, they are people watchers, they like photography, they read a lot, they remember names by a visual hook, they use a checklist to assemble something, and they are concerned with the way they look.

You will be able to place people in this arena by words or phrases they use in their conversation. Here is a small sample of words in this arena:

* that was an eyeful
* beyond a shadow of a doubt
* I see how that can work
* I saw it with my own eyes
* a sight for sore eyes
* what a beautiful sight
* picture perfect
* postcard beautiful
* while looking back

* I can see into the future
* that's a bright idea
* clear as a bell
* seeing is believing
* hindsight is 20-20
* at first glance
* I have a fuzzy idea
* I have a mental picture
* let's see eye to eye
* cast some light on that
* have a bird's eye view
* talk about what we see
* show me what you mean
* in plain sight, etc

Our next system is the auditory system. This system is associated by your sense of sound. People in this system are those that will ask for directions. These people like to talk and listen. They like to have conversations, they would rather listen to the radio than watch TV, they want to listen to a book and not read a book and they want someone to read the instructions on assembly instead of reading the instructions.

You will be able to place people in this arena by words or phrases they use in their conversation. Here is a small sample of words in this arena:

* does it sound OK
* sounds good to me
* I hear what you are saying
* that clicks with me
* hold your tongue
* that sounds like fun
* I got an ear full
* my ears were burning
* she gave me a lot of static
* he said it word for word
* this is what I heard
* I heard it through the grape vine
* within ear shot

* I have something to say
* lend me your ear
* how does that sound to you
* I'd like to suggest something
* describe that in detail
* that's unheard of, etc

The third system is the kinesics system that uses our feelings, emotions and sense of touch. People here like to pet animals, build things with their hands, like to draw, like to touch things and people while talking and they relate to motions and emotions.

Here is a small sample of words in this arena:

* all washed up
* I embrace that idea
* caught on to that
* get in touch with this
* she is hard headed
* he is spineless
* everything went smoothly
* he's tied up right now
* I need a concrete idea
* they had a heated argument
* it boils down to this
* feel it in my bones
* sharp as a tack
* that's bearable
* that rubs me the wrong way
* hang on
* I'm feeling pressured
* feel the wind blowing through your hair
* keep your shirt on
* he's a chip off the old block
* it slipped my mind
* solid as a rock
* pull some strings
* start from scratch, etc

Use this information to establish rapport with people. Once you have, you are on the same plane with them and speak their language. You are NOW just like them and you are in their world. This is how their minds work and you can NOW unlock and control their minds. You are their friend and they like and trust you. Congratulations!

This data came from Steve G. Jones, M.Ed., Clinical Hypnotherapist.

THE MASTER, THE MENTOR, THE MESMERIZING MAN

My first job was with a heating and air conditioning company as a door-to-door canvasser in the year of 1972. Obviously, traditional sales were the norm back then. I share this story with you because my sales instructor used a subtle form of hypnosis and was not aware he was ahead of his time in the field of persuasion.

I had to knock on the homeowner's front door and set appointments for the sales staff. When the homeowner wanted an appointment, they had a choice of morning or afternoon. If they said afternoon, they had a choice of 2:35 or 4:10.

The odd times are out of the norm. People are more likely to remember the strange time.

Did you catch the two KEY points?

The homeowner had a choice of times and the times were odd to leave a lasting impression.

After a few months, I got an opportunity to get into the sales department.

It was at this stage in my career where I learned how to persuade or sell. I was very fortunate to work with an excellent on-the-job trainer, Mr. Richard (Dick) McGinness.

Dick is a master of closing the doors before they are opened. He would nail down resistance before they became an issue. When he got to the end of his persuasion, the homeowners were happy to take care of the paperwork.

Why were the homeowners happy at the close? The homeowners knew they would become happily involved with their new system. A system that is taking care of them day and night.

When Dick would tell the stories and paint the pictures to the homeowners, the homeowners were able to see that beautiful painting Dick just described to the homeowners' sub-conscience minds.

He would always paint the picture using benefits the homeowners will have throughout the next several years with their new member of the family. That new family member is going to keep them cozy and comfortable year round.

Once Dick realized the homeowners are thinking and responding as if they already had the system, Dick would use a word after the benefits. I never heard any other salesperson or speaker use that tiny word.

That very effective and powerful word is "etcetera" (etc). He would sprinkle that word throughout the persuasion. Immediately after he would paint the picture of a benefit or feature and had the couple painting that picture in their minds' eye, he would say "and etc." After he said "etc" he did the critical step of keeping his mouth shut and allowing his future partners to process the solution and paint their own picture in their mind's eye.

Imagine the power Dick had by saying etc at the exact time. He allowed the homeowners to envision their new future. When I said Dick was ahead of his time it was at this stage of the presentation Dick had his future partners in the Alpha state of hypnosis. Neither

Dick nor I knew about hypnosis back then and yet, Dick performed the task perfectly.

He gave the homeowners permission at that point to paint their own picture. A mental picture of comfort, tranquility and enjoying the benefits of having the new family member keeping everyone comfortable all year long.

At the end of the persuasion and ready for the close, he would summarize features, benefits and "etc." He would then say to his future partners, "the only thing left to do is to schedule the arrival of your new family member, which day of the week will work best for you?"

Dick and I still stay in contact to this day and Dick I have four words for you: THANK YOU and etc!

THE BREAKTHROUGH OF GETTING MORE SALES

Persuasion, the act of persuading: act of influencing the mind by arguments and reasons, according to Webster's New Collegiate Dictionary, 1959 edition.

Over 40 years ago, people did think persuasion was an "ACT"; however; in reality, they had the word "ACT" misspelled by one letter.

The word should have been spelled as "ART." It takes knowledge, work and skill to become a successful, powerful and wealthy persuader or solutions specialist.

Persuasion is the key to having what you want, becoming wealthy and having success in any arena. Without persuasion, nothing would get done. The benefit and power of persuasion is the secret of the universe.

Many people have a false impression of persuasion because they feel it is a form of manipulation. When persuasion is used in a wrongful manner, it is a form of manipulation and we do not use it in that form. We use persuasion in the natural form for direction.

People want to be directed in a way that makes them eager and comfortable with taking action on opportunities that benefit them. We all want to better ourselves and will follow the advice of someone that can led us to that end.

Persuasion is about changing the perception of people in order to change their belief and reality. It helps people see things in a different way they did not see before.

Everyone has the ability of persuasion inside of us. Yet, we keep it dormant. Somewhere along our lives' path, by influence from others, our environment or our mental stinkin thinkin, we got the strange idea we are not salespeople, persuaders or solution specialists.

Isn't that weird? That is not beneficial for the quality of our life and the lives of others.

Just think where you could be today if you would have tapped into that resource and used persuasion skills to your advantage. Isn't that an interesting concept?

If you had, what would you do differently than what you are doing today?

Would you be living in a better home? Would you be driving a better car? Would you provide for your family better? Would you go on more vacations? Would you have a better financial plan for you and your family?

Should I continue?

This is the good news. It is not too late for you to sharpen your skills of persuasion to improve your quality of life for yourself, your family and your future partners.

That is important to you, isn't it?

You know you deserve a better quality of life! You do know you can improve your quality of life if you really wanted to do that for yourself and your family.

Doesn't your family deserve a better quality of life?

Then reading through this book, you will pick up some golden nuggets that will do that for you and your family.

AMAZING! START USING THIS NEW TWIST AND WATCH YOUR SALES EXPLODE

Before we get started, it would be helpful to understand the difference between a salesman and a super star salesman. When the words salesman, saleswoman, salesperson and solution specialist are used throughout this book, they all mean the same.

We have gone to stores to buy a certain product that we wanted. When we got to the store, the salesperson walked over to us and tried to "close the sale" immediately. How does that make you feel?

You put up an invisible barrier between yourself and that salesperson, didn't you? He was so pushy that you decided not to buy anything from that person. You probably walked out of that store and went to a different store to buy "the product."

There are many people that call themselves salespeople and they don't have a clue about the process of selling or helping people get what they want. They might as well stand next to the Girl Scouts and ask the same question that they ask. Do you want to buy some Girl Scout cookies? What they should be asking is, "**How many boxes** of girl scout cookies do you want to purchase?" Do not ask a YES or NO question.

The pros know how to relate and guide people into future partners. What's the secret the pros know that you don't know?

The pros listen to their customers, ask questions to gain valuable information and are able to paint pictures in the customers' minds of how that product or service will improve their life. It sounds like an easy process and it actually is an easy process. It's just like getting into Carnegie Hall, all it takes is practice, practice and more practice.

Many people have a problem with this because it requires reprogramming of the way you have been using your words during your lifetime. If you are a newbie, you are lucky because you do not have to reprogram your mind. If there was a way you could use the same words you have used all your life, change a few things that would make a bunch of money, you would be interested, wouldn't you?

You can be assured the amount of investment you made for this book is nothing compared to the amount of money you will receive once you start using your new skills. You can compare your investment as a drop of water is to an ocean.

The best thing about your change is you already have all of the vocabulary you need to become $ucce$$ful as a super star solution specialist. Isn't this getting interesting?

You have to learn how to reformat your presentation. It is the same principle as re-booting your computer to clear the errors and make the machine operate smoothly and efficiently.

The super salespeople, pros or solution specialists use a variation of indirect conversational hypnosis. Don't worry, this will be explained. By using this method, they gain control, acquire attention, trust and confidence that will change the customers' minds and close sales.

You have professions all around you that use the conversational hypnosis techniques. Some of them are:

* Politicians
* Attorneys
* Negotiators
* Counselors
* Doctors
* Healers
* Parents
* Preachers
* Salespeople, etc.

Think of the list of people that use conversational hypnosis and the way they speak. They use the same words as anyone else does and yet they can get people to take action on what it is that the speaker wants. Listen to the way the list of people use their words, the order of the words, the pacing of the words. They use words that are designed to grab and hold your attention and keep you "spellbound" to the end.

Simply stated, conversational hypnosis is indirect communication that affects your perception and thinking and gets your mind in the same frame of thinking as the speaker.

If this is so simple, why is it so little understood?

The reason is until recently, people were able to speak using conversational hypnosis but were unable to teach others how to use conversational hypnosis. Finally the linguists, people who specialize in the study of human language, discovered how the spoken words affect perception and thinking.

Many people have the notion that hypnosis is a form of trickery and the salesperson tricks the customer into buying something the customer does not want, need or can afford. Nothing is further from the truth.

Hypnosis cannot trick anyone into buying a product, bark like a dog or cluck like a chicken if a person does not want to do any of those things. No form of hypnosis can make someone do something against his or her will.

Stage shows and TV gave hypnosis a bad reputation because of the sensationalism. Too many people believe it must be true because I saw it on TV. Every person that got up on the stage was not forced and everyone volunteered to be there.

To this day, many people believe it is a form of sleep when a person is under hypnosis. Not true. You probably have driven home from a hard day at work. You are tired, stressed, agitated and thinking about what to eat for dinner when you realized you are pulling into your driveway.

As you sit in your car, you wonder how did I get here. I don't remember driving home. Guess what? You were in a form of hypnosis. You were in a mild state of hypnosis called the Alpha state of hypnosis. Shocking, isn't it?

Hang on, here's another shocker. Hypnosis is used today to HELP people. The obvious and easiest ones to point out are people that want to lose weight and want to quit smoking. Many people will use hypnosis to reach their goals. Super salespeople, the pros and solution specialists also HELP people by using hypnosis.

You are now beginning to see a trend and how you can use hypnosis to HELP your customers. Oops, I just used some hypnosis on you.

If you have been looking for techniques to increase your ability to influence others, hypnosis is your answer. Of course you have been looking for ways to make more sales; otherwise, you wouldn't be reading this book.

There is no conflict between hypnosis and logical reasoning. Your subconscious will accept what it hears. Hypnosis will enhance the power of imagination but will not override logic and reason.

There are different levels of hypnosis and you are probably in one or more levels every day. Hypnosis is a natural state and you move in and out of this throughout each day. Many of your everyday normal activities are performed under hypnosis without you being aware of it. When you are daydreaming, we know you do, you are in light hypnosis.

Have you ever been to a bookstore that has the coffee shop within the store? If so, you have seen people reading a book and they have an intense look in their eyes and outside noise or distractions don't seem to bother them. They are in light hypnosis.

You are now reading a fascinating book and you are unaware of your outside distractions because you are focused on the printed words. Your mind has slowed slightly, your focus is narrow, your breathing is slow and you are relaxed. Yep, you too are in the Alpha mode of hypnosis. Said another way, you are in a light form of hypnosis as you read this.

The deepest form of hypnosis is called hypnotic amnesia and a person cannot remember what happened during hypnosis and their imagination is greatly increased.

This is the level of hypnosis Doctors use for childbirth, minor surgery and dental procedures. The good news for us as sales people is we do not have to use hypnotic amnesia.

You, like most people, use your words in a direct fashion, don't you? You will now change the order of your words to make irresistible suggestions. If your words are irresistible, how can anyone say anything other than YES? Makes dollars, doesn't it?

Your suggestions are used to set up expectations for your future partners and their thoughts can become self-fulfilling truths. You will alter or change your presentation to have the right choice and order of words to create a change in the way people think.

To word this differently, you will create a script for your presentation. Just think about the speeches the President gives to the nation or anyone; every speech is a script. The best of the best get together to write the script and ensure every word is the proper word and in the proper place to hypnotize his audience. You however, do not need to know your script verbatim. You need to know your script well enough to alter the content to fit the needs of your future partners.

A $ucce$$ful salesperson, like you will become, understands the psychology of verbal and non-verbal suggestions. Your income is based on the quality of your verbal suggestions. The suggestions you give to your customers are presented in such a logical and subtle way the customers feel as though they bought the product and were not sold.

You, in the past, probably sold using direct suggestions, which caused your customers to put up their defensive barrier between you and them. Once you master the irresistible suggestions, they will seem invisible on the surface, eliminate the defensive barriers and create a positive impact on their subconscious.

As a solution specialist, you know you must create rapport with your future partners to make a sale. Part of rapport is trust. Happy days are here because hypnotic selling builds trust quickly.

It's an improvement on what you have been doing for a long time. Yes, you probably are apprehensive about changing habits and systems. The good news is this, after you change and feel the new process is second nature to you, you will want to thank me for the change.

Top solution specialists know how to trigger hypnotic trust. You will never be able to help people until you have their trust. You have met someone that you liked and trusted immediately without any reason or justification. It works because the other person says or does something that reminds you subconsciously of someone you have trusted and liked for a long time.

Trust is critical in hypnosis because it creates a suggestible state of mind for reducing resistance. Trust gives us power and a massive communication shortcut in existence. You need to build trust quickly.

Use magical words to get your future partners senses involved. Your words can place your future partners in another world of sights, sounds, smell, touch, hearing and feelings. This is called ideosensory trance and we experience it daily. Go to any business that sells a major product and the pro salesperson will use words to make you feel as though you are part of the product.

Buying a car is a good example. The salesperson will have you project yourself into the future driving your car and feeling how it handles, corners, accelerates, stops, the smell of the leather seats, the sound of the awesome radio with the 20 speakers and the attention you will get when you drive past your friends in your shiny new red convertible.

The salesperson has you doing all of this before you even take a test drive. You already bought the car before your butt was in the seat. The salesman filled your wants and he sold you on the benefits and your emotions and you "bought" the car.

That was an example of using ideosensory trance with positive emotions. You can also use ideosensory trance to trigger negative emotions and create a sale. How can this happen?

Imagine you live in an area that recently had many burglaries and your home does not have an alarm system. The solution specialist comes to your home, measures the square footage, designs a system for your home and shares how many homes were broken into within your area.

He is selling you on security and not losing your belongings and avoiding damage to your home. It is selling to avoid the negative. Other markets that use this approach are:

* Insurance sales; accident, health, fire, theft, auto etc
* Maintenance programs; big items like your car or home
* Health clubs; to avoid that flabby look
* Car sales; to stop driving that unsafe broken down clunker, etc

One more type of hypnosis is amnesia. Yes, it is what you think, getting your customers to forget. This is common in daily events and sales. Have you ever forgotten a person's name or address? You probably said, "My mind went blank." You had temporarily gone into a hypnotic state and left the real world. When you came back to the real world, you had no memory of where you were.

The sales pros have an ability to activate this forgetting response in their customers when discussing your competitor's product. This works best for customers that are not detail-oriented.

An example is a competitor who tells all the nuts and bolts about his product and gets the customer overwhelmed. You come on the scene and the future partner shares that information with you. All you need to say is "it's easy to forget about all of those insignificant steps involved with that product when you realize how easy my product operates."

If you have to work with a detail-oriented customer, do not try to eliminate those details. Find out what the details are and then explain how they can get more of what they like with your product. You say, "it is easy to forget about all the facts, figures, data and claims with the other product and my product is so simple to use you will remember it easily." Use hypnotic amnesia to erase memories of insignificant details.

Oh, I know what you are thinking now. What if I want my future partners to remember? You use the opposite method, which is called hypernesia. This is a method to enhance memory and recall. When you use hypernesia, the first thing you do is tell your future partners what they will remember. You are placing pictures in their minds that they cannot forget.

Use anchor words and phrases like:

- You will think about this all day long.
- This will be the last thing you think about as you fall asleep.
- It's unforgettable.
- You will remember this for the rest of your life.
- This is going to leave you with a positive memory forever.
- You won't be able to forget.
- When you watch TV you will think about this. Etc

The techniques used in hypnosis selling are not only powerful and effective; they are used in an ethical and non-threatening atmosphere. You want your future partners in a relaxed, open minded, receptive and positive mindset before, during and after your offering.

A key element in getting your customer in that emotional state is to ask him or her to reflect back to an earlier time to a place where they were happy, safe, at ease and in a positive emotional situation. This process is called revivication where people relive earlier experiences.

You can ask them to describe the first toy they bought and how they felt about that transaction. Your customers will go back to all the positive emotions associated with that experience.

When the customer describes the positive emotions from earlier times, you can share with them that is exactly how you are going to feel when you own your product.

That will induce a buying signal for your customer. You have placed them into an altered state of awareness. They NOW want to buy and have those positive feelings again.

We have gone through different forms of hypnosis and the benefits of those forms. Having done that has placed your mind into a different mindset on hypnosis than it was when you started reading this book.

Your mind will now accept the framework of hypnosis. All hypnosis is nothing more than suggestions as described above. Hypnosis is just manipulating the consciousness and allows a person to become aware of the suggestions.

When someone is in the Alpha state of hypnosis, they are 200 times more suggestible to your words. These suggestions take on a journey and their imagination becomes deeper and more vivid along that journey. The suggestions are received from verbal, non-verbal and body language messages.

Think of hypnosis as a game of fantasy and make belief. No one can hypnotize someone into doing something he or she doesn't want to do which means all hypnosis is self-hypnosis. The persuader just helps people into that state of mind.

The pro can take you on a mental journey by describing experiences and you will reflect on your experiences while you are listening. You will go to a pleasant and happy time in your past and associate that experience with the information the persuader is giving you. Your subconscious mind does not distinguish between what is real and the imaginary.

This is a key point for the solution specialists. They want you to stay in that positive mental state for a long time because you will start to experience its effects in reality. You are in a mild waking trance and engaged in the story just like you are when you watch a great movie. The way you think is what you create in your world.

THE TRUTH ABOUT HABITS

We are creatures of habit.

It takes 21 days to break a habit.

You have a waste paper basket on the left side of your desk and now move it to the right side of your desk. After you moved the basket, you will continue to throw discarded paper in the basket on the left side. After you realized there is no basket on the left side, you pick up the paper and throw it into the basket on the right side of your desk.

After you read this book, you have a choice to make.

You can put the book down and continue to do what you have been doing day in and day out. If that is you and you expect different results from reading this book, then you my friend are the definition of insanity.

Doing the same thing over and over and expecting different results. Not going to happen!

If you don't make changes you are in a rut and a rut is nothing more than a grave with both ends kicked out. You don't want to be in the grave so get your butt out of there and make things happen.

The other choice is to NOW make changes by learning some of the golden nuggets and use the knowledge to improve your quality of life. Which one sounds better to you?

You already have the knowledge and skills to do this and it just takes a realignment of your stinkin thinkin and a "get 'er done" mindset.

Is it worth 21 days of your life to make a small change in your habits if it will improve the lifestyle for you and your family?

If you are committed to getting a different mindset, I'm sure you will realize positive results in less than 21 days.

Remember, it is just small changes you need to make for big rewards.

You have your destination in your mind's eye. You know the route you need to take to reach your destination. Situations will arise along the path that will cause you to make adjustments to stay on course. Just a little tweak here and there and you will be successful.

Where are you going today?

Where are you going tomorrow?

Where are you going five years from today?

You need to know your destination before you start the journey.

In a moment, you will receive some skills and techniques that will allow your mindset to change for the better.

Once you start learning the skills and techniques, you will know you are getting:

* smarter
* more powerful
* unstoppable and getting your life in order

After you have learned and use the skills and techniques, you will be able to see, feel and enjoy the fruits of your labor. You will realize how much your life is NOW improving.

You NOW feel good about yourself and you NOW know you deserve the finer things in life, don't you?

Your journey on the road to success takes dedication, time and work and you may have bumps in the road. If you get down in the dump during the journey you just need to **give yourself a checkup from the neck-up to get rid of your stinkin thinkin and prevent hardening of the attitudes.**

A positive attitude is critical for this journey. I know you can and will do this, right? Then let's begin.

READY

SET

GO!!

DISCOVER YOUR SWEET SPOT

You and I know if we are going to persuade someone to our product or service, it is always more effective and easier to share information with our niche group. In addition, it is always easier to persuade to our future partners that want and need our product or service.

Makes sense, doesn't it? I like to say, NO, it makes dollars!

Today, with the internet we are taught to find out what our people want and provide the product to them.

That sounds simple enough. That is your niche market.

You set an appointment with a person for storm windows and when you got to the home, you discovered he is not the homeowner. He is the renter and you are in the wrong market.

This is an excellent example of knowing who is your niche market.

In the internet arena, you email to your name list and conduct a survey to learn what they want.

When you get the survey back, you compile the data and the item that has the most replies is your niche market.

If you do not have what they want, you create it or get someone to create it for you. You then provide that to your name list and your pockets will be full of money.

We call that group of people you helped your niche market and they will become your future partners for life.

Since we are talking about the internet arena, let's spend some time discussing the entrepreneurs within that arena. Entrepreneurs, I am one, are people who are free thinkers and do not like or perform well within the traditional structured business arena.

The typical 8 to 5, Monday through Friday, punch the time clock scenario does not fit the DNA of an entrepreneur and that makes them practically unemployable. Instead of getting a paycheck from an 8 to 5 job, they create their own business to be their own boss and earn a very respectable income. They want freedom more than profit.

They generally resent authority figures and do not like to take orders from people they feel are no better or smarter than they. They have a self-driven attitude and desire to start their business and not work for a business. They don't accept other people's decision-making choices and they want to make their own decisions.

Entrepreneurs perform to the beat of a different drummer. Knowing this, you must present your product or service using the beat of a different drummer. You must present your solutions with a practical, street smart, specifically designed offer for each entrepreneur that will enhance his or her business.

Entrepreneurs are like fingerprints, each one is unique and you must adapt your solution to each unique entrepreneur. At least, make him feel like your solution is unique. Be sure to use the KISS (keep it simple salesman) approach because the entrepreneur does not care about the theory of your solution, just how to use your solution.

Do not use traditional old school words when your share your solution with the entrepreneur. Here is a list of buzzwords to use:

* We are adaptable and flexible.
* We understand.
* We are helpful.
* We are thorough.
* We leave no stone uncovered.
* We do whatever it takes.
* We work with your business procedures.
* We are here to help you and your business.

When you begin to share your solution and use the words of being flexible, accountable, helpful, etc., you give the perception of being willing to do whatever it takes to enhance the entrepreneur's business. This sets you apart from the other "salespeople" because it shows you too are unique.

You and the entrepreneur are on the same plane because both of you are unique. You now have a bond with the entrepreneur. Your next statement should be along the line of saying your product or service will supply more order and control, plus reduce any chaos like the other products or service on the market today.

The entrepreneur, like any other person, needs to hear and understand the value of your product or service before you share the investment. However, most entrepreneurs feel like a purchase is from their personal account, unlike a large corporation, because the entrepreneur's business is an extension of his personal live.

You should present the investment in a street form before you give the amount. Phrases like "it doesn't cost anymore than a steak dinner" or "anymore than going to the movies" or "anymore than what you make on three additional sales" will resonate the entrepreneur.

By this time you and the entrepreneur have a bond and a working relationship. He should become happily involved with your product or service at this point in time. However, if he wants to get comparisons or look into another person's offer, don't fear. Remember, never say anything negative about any type of competition.

However, you can use words to describe the other "offers" that will keep the entrepreneur from buying from the other guy.

These words are actuate to describe other businesses; however, they have a negative connotation to the mindset of an entrepreneur:

- Traditional business procedures
- Structured policies
- Employee based
- Organizational structure
- Theory based business
- Regulation bonded
- Same for everyone
- Uniformed approach for all

All of these words or phrases are great and there is nothing negative about any one of them; however, they do not set well with a free spirited entrepreneur person.

HOW ENTRANCING STORIES AND METAPHORS HELP YOUR BOTTOM LINE

Suppose a person comes to you for advice about how to become happily involved within the sales arena. Would you paint a picture for him of a Bed of Roses by saying things like?

* It is easy.
* Anyone can do it.
* No problems.
* A piece of cake.
* No sweat.

Wouldn't that give a person the wrong picture to put into his or her mind? They may go into the sales arena with false expectations and hope.

Maybe you are a straight shooter and you tell things like they are. You lay everything on the table by saying things like:

- It is hard work.
- Most people fail at this business.
- It takes years of training and dedication to be $ucce$$ful.
- Less than 10% of the people stay in the business.

When you use that approach, how likely is that person going to pursue the sales career? Some people can't handle the truth. Even though you were truthful, you probably would scare that person away from an outstanding career.

There is a way to be truthful and less threatening to convey your message and help that person into the sales business. You should share truthful information and use positive sales stories to motivate that person into the sales business.

A good way to do this is to use a comparison of building a house to building a sales business.

We all live in a building, a house, an apartment, a condo, a sky-scraper, etc. We all know that the building had to be built from the ground up.

The roof is not built before the walls are in place and the walls can't be built before the foundation is completed. Everyone knows a building needs a solid foundation for security.

Some of the hardest, dirtiest and most time consuming part of the building is the foundation phase. Isn't it strange the foundation requires all of this and then it gets covered with dirt and no one will see the efforts required to build that foundation?

Use this example as an analogy or metaphor between building a home, a skyscraper or any building and building a solid business. People can accept the work involved with constructing a building and then will relate those same ideas and principles to building their sales business with a positive mindset and a can do attitude. They know that you told them the truth about their new business and they now trust you more than before.

Another great benefit in using metaphors is that it creates a C.Y.A. (cover your assets) for you. When your person starts his or her journey into building a sales business, they may encounter some building challenges.

If a person faces a sales building challenge, he can reflect on the metaphor of constructing a skyscraper and realize there were challenges during the building stage of the skyscraper and that building did get completed. This will reinforce the person's attitude of "I can and will do this." Positive reinforcements are good!

Congratulations, you just discovered the hidden value of story telling and metaphors. In fact, stories, analogies and metaphors are the glue that holds together the value of hypnosis and sales methods.

Reflect to a time when you were at church and the preacher was giving the sermon using stories, analogies and metaphors. As you sat there listening you got the feeling that the preacher was talking directly with you and no one else in the church.

That, my friend, is a pro at using stories to get you into a medium trance of hypnosis. You never realized you were hypnotized while you were in church, did you?

All sales pros use metaphors, stories and analogies and that is why they are pros!

A pro will use these techniques in an enjoyable and interesting manner and yet they are extremely powerful. The reason for using stories is the fact that you can use hidden commands or suggestions within the stories that you cannot use as well when you speak directly to your customer.

The customer hears the story and learns that John Doe did this or that so I can now do this or that. Think of it as a monkey hear, monkey do scenario. Sorry, that was an analogy, wasn't it?

Here are a few advantages of story telling:

- They place you in the story from your past experiences.
- They keep your future partners attention longer.
- You can address key points that could not be discussed directly.
- You can use the most powerful forms of hypnotic selling.

* You can make an innate object become humanlike.
* Stories create a greater value with a higher level of salesmanship when you discuss features and enhance benefits.
* They give creditability to you and your product or service.
* They do more than entertain, they leave a lasting memory.
* They are highly effective in sharing information and instructing.
* The future partner has a higher awareness, understanding and insight of your product or service.
* They allow your future partner to take a learned experience from one area of their life into another area of their life.
* The future partner adapts the story to fit his own needs and that gives more value to your product or service.
* They allow the future partner to paint their own unique picture of how their life will improve with your product or service.
* The time goes by much quicker for the future partner and you. Etc.

From the information you NOW know about stories, when is the best time to use stories? "Yes," is the answer. Do not wait until you are near the end of your presentation to share your stories. You will fit into the "too little, too late" cliché.

You need to have an arsenal of stories in your toolbox and be able to pull out the story you need to fit the demands of your presentation on the spot. The pros, you are getting there, use stories throughout their presentation. You should too!

How many stories do your need in your toolbox? Think of your toolbox as a bottomless cup of coffee and you can never fill your cup. The time you believe you have all the stories you will need, a situation will arise and bite you in the butt because you didn't have a story for the issue. You need to think and act like a Boy Scout and "Be Prepared."

Here is an important point; you must write all of your stories. After you have written your story, you NOW need to script your story or message into a powerful, non-threatening hypnosis picture for your future partners.

You should write, revise, rehearse, review, revise, and do the wash and rinse routine until you have it as near to perfection as you can. The proof in the pudding will come when you are presenting your presentation to your future partners. You do not need to memorize every word but you do need to know the content.

After your presentation and away from your partners, write notes on the good, the bad and the really ugly. Find a quiet place and revise your presentation again. Remember the wash and rinse routine? You must do this over, and over, and over; you get the picture, don't you?

Knowing when to use stories in your presentation is crucial. Knowing what type of story to share is even more crucial. You want your presentation to flow from the beginning to the end and make complete sense throughout the entire presentation. Below is a cash-list (checklist) of the types of stories to share:

* Introductory Stories
* Attention-Getting
* Product Information
* Overcoming Fears
* Money, money, money
* Ego-enhancement
* Improved Productivity
* Family-Unity
* Security
* Closing

Introductory stories are "I" stories. Share with your future partners who you are, why you are there and how you helped many people in the past.

Attention getting stories grab people's attention and why they should focus on your product or service. They tell the customers why they should listen to you and your offer.

Attention getting stories tell more than features and benefits. They sprinkle that information throughout the presentation in a format that is interesting instead of boring.

Overcoming fear stories tell how other people had the same fears and their fears were unjustified.

Money stories inform people how they can afford your product and they are losing money because they do not own your product. These stories also inform the future partners how your product will save money and may earn money.

Ego-enhancement stories show how other people that invested in your product had their self-confidence, pride and self-esteem increased. They also show how people will respect you and act as if you are the authority figure once you own the product or service.

Improved productivity explains how your product or service has improved the efficiency of other businesses by reducing downtime, increasing output and decreasing mistakes and errors.

Family unity stories share how families become closer after using your product or service.

Security stories allow people to have peace of mind knowing their belongings are safe and their financial security is safe.

Closing sales stories are a summary of the benefits your product or service provides. This is where the storytelling gets your future partners into the buying mode.

Story telling and metaphors entertain and relax your future partners and leave a lasting memory in picture format within your future partners' minds.

The Process

We can sum up the procedures of telling a story by using the example of constructing a building and we will use your home as the example. You set an appointment with the architect to get his professional advice of creating a plan to transform your dreams into a reality of creating your home. You are NOW in the **connecting, rapport and trusting phase** of the process.

This is a very important phase because you will decide if you like the person, trust the person and will want to work with the person that has the skills and knowledge to help you reach your goals of constructing your home.

The architect will ask what types of homes you lived in and what you liked about each home. He is getting information that is interesting to you and learning what you like and would probably want in your new home.

You are going back in time to your past homes and only sharing information that made you happy with each home and he is getting you into a positive state of mind. When you are in this mindset, you are more likely to give the architect valuable information because you feel as if he is a friend that is going to help you.

You are actually in the Alpha stage of hypnosis and the architect as taken you into the **information phase** of the process.

The architect will keep asking questions of what you want and why each want is important for you. This will uncover the benefits, features, design, appearance and functionality in your new home.

He is collecting important bits of information so he can construct the perfect home for your needs, wants and desires. It is the same process as finding all the pieces of a jigsaw puzzle and putting them in the proper order to create the finished puzzle.

During the information phase, the architect may know of a better solution to one of your ideas and he will ask if you have ever thought of designing a particular room this way instead of the way you described the room. He is helping you to make the right choices by giving suggestions for you to create your perfect home. You are getting more involved with the process of selling yourself on his advice and you will feel like you are the one that made that particular decision.

After he has all the information he needs to design the perfect home for you, he will ask if you would like to see what your new home will look like. He just let you into the **presentation phase of the process.**

This is the phase where the architect stands out as the solution specialist. He will share stories of how other people had the same experiences that you had with your other homes and how he helped them get what they wanted in their new home. He said how he presented the plans of the new home with other people and went over all the details of the plans and the people decided to take action to construct their new dream home and are happy with the results.

He is building his credibility and letting you know he is a professional in his arena. You met with him having a vision in your mind's eye of your new dream home and he will be able to transform your vision into a reality. At this point in time, you realize he is the person that will make things happen and you take action on getting happily involved with his expertise and allow him to start the process of construction for your new dream home. He has just taken you through the **commitment phase** of the process.

This is the process to take when you are speaking with your future partners. Each phase builds into the next phase until you reach the end and people take action on your advice. All you are doing is asking questions throughout your presentation and giving suggestions or advice on what worked for people that had the same issues as the people you are speaking with. It's the same structure with different messages.

Name and describe the 4 phases of the story telling process

1. _____

2. _____

3. _____

4. _____

The 4 Phases of story telling

Rapport and Trusting Phase

This is when you gain the trust of the people and they become your friends. Once you have their trust, they will open up to you and share what their pain is so you can create a solution to their issues.

Information Phase

You find out all the information needed in this phase to create the solution to their problems. You share with them how you had other people having similar issues and how you helped them resolve those issues.

Presentation Phase

This is the time you describe the solution to your future partners' issues. You ask them how they feel about your solution and if they feel like it will work for them when they decide to take action on your solution.

Commitment Phase

Now is the time for your future partners to fish or cut bait. This is the time they make the commitment to get happily involved with your solution to their issues.

DISCOVER HOW TO GET ENTHUSIASTIC PARTNERS

You need to know what the future partners' needs are before you can solve their pain. Two different people will most likely have two different needs. Your main goal at this time is to learn the pain and the WHY for the pain before you can customize a solution for their pain.

You learn what the needs are by asking questions. Many salespeople fail to ask questions at the proper time. Too many will ask questions too soon within the presentation and have not established any rapport with their customer.

We know that information gathering creates rapport and that should involve 90% of your presentation. This is the time where you are the "friend" and there to solve your friends' pain.

You started your presentation or warm up as soon as you met your future partners by asking the three general questions which they answered "YES." PERFECT! You now have their mind conditioned to say "YES" and they now have a positive mindset. Your three questions can be about anything as long as they will get a "YES" response.

Ask general questions to learn if they know anything about your product or service. For example, if you were marketing widgets you could ask if they know anything about widgets.

If they know nothing about widgets, you may want to ask why they wanted to talk with you about widgets. If one of their friends recommended you to your future partners, you now have credibility and you are perceived as a widget expert.

If they do know about widgets, chances are they are looking at other people that market widgets. After they share with you they have knowledge about widgets, you should ask what they know about widgets and who else are they looking at for a widget.

Ask if they ever owned a widget. If they have owned a widget, ask how that made them feel once they became happily involved with their widget. They will share with you how happy they were the day they received their widget and all the benefits they received by owning a widget.

Take them back to the day they acquired their widget and ask of all of the benefits, which one they like the best. After they tell you which one the like the best, you ask why. Their answer could lead you into another question that does not pertain directly to the widget. Ask of all the benefits, which one made you feel the happiest. Once again, ask why after they answer.

You now have some substance from the past that you can and should use for the present and project into the future. The key points of information that helped you ask more targeted questions are the ones that made them feel happy and the ones they liked the best. Build on the positive emotions and feelings they received in the past with their widget.

Ask your future partners if they could redesign a widget, are there any benefits they would want that their other widget did not provide. If they would build a widget that would provide more benefits, then your widget should provide those benefits for your future partners.

Ask them why they feel like it is time to acquire another widget today. If they don't feel like today is a good time to get another widget, ask them when would be good time in their plan to get another widget.

If they don't have a specific time, you do not have a qualified "prospect" and you must now make a decision to stay or to leave and find a qualified "prospect." It's your choice; however, time is money.

If your future partners tell you that their widget is inoperative and today is a good time to acquire another widget, you now have qualified future partners.

From your questions you learned the widget they bought lasted 18 years. Take your future partners back 18 years to the day they purchased their widget and have them tell you how happy they felt when they owned their first and only widget.

As they share their feelings you will notice their eyes will light up and they will start to smile. This is the time for you to share with them how special that widget was and how much the widget became part of their daily lives.

You now say that you may know of a solution of having them feel as good as and even better than the day they acquired their widget.

You just aroused their curiosity and they will ask you to share with them the solution. You will now share the improvements made in the widget industry and how much your widget has improved over the widgets of the past 18 years.

You will say phrases like "you're going to love your new widget because that little guy has tripled the benefits of your other widget." "In fact, your new widget will out perform your original widget and accomplish your chores in one fourth the time it took your other widget to complete the tasks."

The life expectancy of your new widget has tripled which means your little guy will be with you for more than three decades. Once you start using the little guy, you will wonder how you got along before without him.

Mr. and Mrs. Future Partners, can you even imagine in your wildest dreams, how happy you will be with your new member of the family? Oh, I know how excited you are to get him here as soon as you can, aren't you? What day should I deliver your new family member, Tuesday or Wednesday?

Now is the time for you to SHUT UP and let the subconscious mind transfer to the conscious mind for processing and decide on a delivery day. Once your future partners give you the day they want the little guy at home, you start the paper work for delivery.

You are a problem solver, a solution specialist and a super star salesman professional. Nothing happens until a sale is made and you are the type of person that makes things happen.

NOTICE!
THE HARD WAY
OR THE EASY WAY

There are two types of questions you may ask your future partners.

You may ask direct questions or indirect questions. Which type do you use? Which type causes your prospects to resist giving answers? Which type causes your future partners to answer with quality information that can help you in closing?

We know interrogators in police departments use the form of direct questions. How do their "clients" usually respond to the questions?

The interrogation process can and usually takes a long time because the "client" does not want to give any truthful answers. Most everyone has seen TV shows that portray this scenario. Even your future partners have seen this on TV.

Your job, as a solution specialist, is to get answers to your questions so you know what product or service you can offer your future partners to fill their needs. This is the time that separates the men from the boys. Said another way, are you a salesman or a super star solution specialist?

A salesman is there to fill his customers needs by selling his product or service. He knows he must establish rapport so he uses some small talk and goes directly into his sales presentation.

He had not scripted his presentation so he starts by asking questions to his customers to get information. He did not do the proper setup for gaining rapport and his customers do not trust him.

The customers will give the same quality of answers that the "client" gives the interrogator on TV. The customers put up the invisible barrier of resistance and the salesman does not get a sale.

The super star solution specialist (pro) knows some information about his future partners, spends time getting to know them better, and is complimentary about their home and personal items.

He spends time becoming a friend with his future partners. The pro will use indirect questions to get the information he needs to complete the sale.

After he learns the WHY behind the need, the solution specialist will say something to the effect of "I don't know what you hope to gain by having my product or service?" After he gets their answer he will ask, "why would that be important for you?"

Forming questions in this manner by using indirect questions, you turn the tables on your future partners. You put them in the foreground of selling you the reason why they need your product and why you should "allow them to become happily involved with your product."

This is a great way to have your future partners become the salespeople and you are an order-taker. Some people call this method the surprise approach. It is really the intelligent and non-threatening approach.

Most people are use to the salesman trying to sell, sell and sell and not asking; "why do you want this," "I don't know what you want" and "I don't know what kind of income you have" to name a few. People rarely object to indirect questions and objections are common with direct questions.

Non-verbal language or body language used with indirect questions is very powerful. When you use this method another one of your senses is being used.

Your future partners not only hear your message, they also see your gestures and body movements. If you make a statement and you want them to agree with you, start shaking your head up and down. That will cause a positive response from your future partners.

You can turn a statement into a question by simply raising your hand, raising an eyebrow in a questioning posture or an upturned hand. These gestures are called "sales artistry" and they add visual interest to a simple verbal message.

The pros have a special talent, technique or skill that separates them from other salespeople. The solution specialists have situation awareness and use that to help read future partners. Many people believe the pros are mind readers and intuitive.

The pros do an outstanding job of asking mind reading questions and statements. How do they get proficient with this skill?

The pros create an intuitive link or special understanding between themselves and their future partners. Once that link is established, it becomes much easier to influence them to your product or service.

The future partners feel like the solution specialist will take care of their needs and a relationship of friendship and trust has been developed on a higher level than before.

The solution specialist will establish the intuitive link by mirroring the future partners' wants, needs, views, values and tastes. The future partners feel like the solution specialist can almost read their minds.

The pro does this by observing the people and their surroundings. He studies his future partners' mannerisms, gestures, tonality, posture, facial expressions, hairstyle, hands and clothing.

He gathers all of the information and then makes statements that are general and can apply to many people. While he makes these statements, he puts feelings and sincerity into his speech. Doing this causes his future partners to feel like he knows the family inside out.

Here are a few general statements:

- You impress me as a person that tries to provide for his family.
- I can see you are a practical person.
- It is obvious you try to take care of your health.

The generalized questions can apply to most people; however, your future partners feel as though you know a lot about them and they will take down their defense barriers because you are a friend that will not try to sell something that they don't want.

Start writing generalized questions that fit your sales presentation. If you are having trouble creating the questions or thinking of the material, go to your newspaper and look at the astrology column.

You do not have to believe in astrology to use the material. The statements in the astrology section are generalized statements and they will get your brain working for generalized statements that you will create for your presentation.

When you properly build rapport and ask the right questions, your future partners will give you the information you need to get them happily involved with your product or service.

You learned how important it is to script your stories. That is true and there is another very important area that needs to be discussed and that information will allow you to earn more cash than you have ever earned in the same area before. You are interested in learning how to improve your cash flow, aren't you?

The pros use a critical tool that produces more cash than the average salesperson earns. That tool cannot be purchased because it is a unique tool that the solution specialist creates. He creates the tool and it is his sales script book.

Sales presentations are like fingerprints; no two are alike. The same is said for the closing of sales. Every solution specialist has his own style and every close is unique. The content used by one solution specialist will produce a sale and may not produce a sale for a different solution specialist.

This is one reason why every sales script book will be unique. Your custom designed sales script book addresses your style of closing sales.

The sales script sales book is an organized set of the most powerful and useful ways of handling the exact objections and resistance you get in your sales calls. It addresses the specific reasons why your future partners do not want to buy at that moment. The book does not address generalities or theories about sales.

Research has proven that the solution specialist will have up to 100% more sales than the non-pro salesman. It is worth your time and effort to create your own sales script book and double your sales volume, isn't it?

Research also has shown us that creating your own sales script book will improve many more of your sales skills. You get better at building trust by improving your pacing, telling mesmerizing stories, using attention focusing statements, asking powerful sales questions and trigger words that allow your future partners to want to buy. In short, they are powerful and they create sales.

What is your sales script book? It is your book created and designed by you. It is your velvet hammer for closing. Think of it as your pre-briefing guide prior to your presentation and your de-briefing report after your presentation.

It is your book that contains the most powerful and $ucce$$ful phrases or scripts you use to counter any resistance and close the sale. It is the nuts and bolts of getting that sale. It must be organized into sections of different objections with the solutions and the book should become your sales bible and with you at all times.

A few minutes before every presentation, glance over the areas you feel you may encounter with the next presentation. Read your responses and that will plant in your sub-conscious mind the proper action to take during the presentation. The information is NOW fresh in your mind.

An example of this is you having an appointment where you and your future partners are face-to-face, such as an in-home one-call closing situation. You made the appointment and learned from setting the appointment the people may have issues with price, service and warranty of your product.

You have your sales script book at your side and you stop your car five minutes from the future partners' home. You have done your job properly and you have your book divided into sections. You read the sections called Price, Service and Warranty and you are now ready to go into the home and get them happily involved with your product.

After your presentation and away from your partners, go over the area you used during the close to reinforce your quality of performance. If you learned a new tactic during the presentation, write the new information in your book at this time so you will have that tactic for the next time you need it. Your book should be as big as you need it to be for your presentations.

You may now be thinking you don't have enough information to write a sales script book. Don't worry, be happy! Since you are reading this and absorbing the information, you are way ahead of the average salesperson.

Your book is designed to fill your needs and it does not have to be huge. You will add to your book all the time because it is a process that never stops.

When you quit learning new things, it is time for someone to bury you. You are dead even though you are still breathing. A small sales script book is better than no sales script book.

Your sales book will not be created overnight because you are always adding new information to the book. That information is unique to you and will work well for you. It may not work for anyone else. You have to approach this the same way you would eat an elephant: take it one bite at a time.

Example of a Sales Script Book

ISSUE: *It costs too much*

RESPONSE: Repeat "costs too much" and shut up. Let them explain exactly what it is that cost too much. Find out the real issue. They may say something such as the down payment, total investment, monthly investment, length of term for payments or something else is an issue for them.

Once they share the real reason you can share some creative financing for them to take advantage of the offer. You may have longer payment options, smaller down payment, discount for paying in full, take payment of multiple credit cards or any other methods you may want to use. Then ask, "Which method works best for you?"

ISSUE: *I can't buy the entire package*

RESPONSE: Which part of the package is most important for you at this time? How would having that part of the package help you NOW?

How long would it take you to complete that part of the package? After you finished that part of the package, you do want to have the next part of the package, don't you? If you could design a method of having all of the parts to the package and make the investment to fit your financial account, how would you design that scenario? Let them tell you how they want to secure the parts of the package and do custom financing to fit their schedule.

EVERYTHING BEGINS WITH THOUGHT

Everything begins with thought. This book began with a thought.

It was written just for you.

What kind of thoughts do you have?

Random or controlled?

Is your mind a wandering generality or a walking specific?

Studies have shown highly effective people, the super salespeople, the solution specialists have controlled thoughts. While others have random thoughts.

Our thoughts can be controlled. People that control their thoughts get what they want.

That sounds great, don't you agree?

Every thought has a psychosomatic response. Ok, that means everything you think in your mind causes your body to respond, some to the mind and some to the body. (by Marshall Sylver)

It is possible while you are persuading people, some things you say will cause them to reject what you said. And some things you say will cause them to become happily involved with your product or service.

That, my friend, is the power of the spoken words you chose for your persuasion.

An example of this would be for you to imagine you are walking past a lemon grove. You see a tree full of ripe lemons and you pluck the biggest and ripest lemon from the tree.

As you pull the lemon from the tree, you can feel the bumpy texture of the lemon peel and smell that distinct citrus smell only a lemon can expel. It smells great!

You then take your pocketknife and cut a slit into the lemon peel. You cut completely around that lemon which causes some juice to run into your hands.

The smell is now more intense as the juice leaks out of the lemon.

You have triggered three of your senses at this point in time.

You now push your thumbs into the lemon pulling it in half.

The juice is running all over your hands.

You take one half of the lemon, tilt your head back as far as you can and squeeze the lemon half into your mouth.

As you do, some lemon juice is running on the outside of your mouth and the rest is running inside your mouth.

As the juice from the lemon hits your tongue, your senses and taste buds are energized and you taste that tartness of the lemon.

Your mouth puckers and the nerves in your neck muscles tighten. That is normal when you get your first bite of something sour.

But oooh, that lemon tastes sooo good!

If you like lemons, you enjoyed this story about lemons.

Your mind placed you in that story so you could experience the effects of the lemon juice without having the lemon juice.

Powerful, isn't it?

On the other hand, if you do not like lemons, you wanted the story to be over as soon as possible. In fact, you didn't even want to read the lemon story.

Yes, words are powerful and you will pull your prospects closer to you or push them away.

Know as much about your prospects as you can. You need to know what story to share with them during your persuasion.

You need to know how to turn that lemon into lemonade.

That is done by using the correct words.

You are ready to learn the skill NOW.

The more informed and educated you are in this arena, the more $ucce$$ful you will become.

5 GROUPS OF WORDS THAT COMMAND RESULTS

Words, when used properly, are very powerful instruments and vehicles that can take you from where you are today to your destiny tomorrow. Some words are in a class all their own and can provide positive results for you and your future partners when you use them for the betterment of mankind.

You NOW know that we want our future partners in the Alpha stage, or light stage of hypnosis, because their minds are 200 times more receptive to our words.

In a moment, you will learn some of the key words to use that will get your future partners in the Alpha stage. After you used the "words" and have your future partners in the Alpha stage, their minds are open and they are focused directly on what you are sharing with them.

There are five groups of Alpha Power Patterns and each pattern has specific words within that group.

Envision now in your mind's eye a pyramid constructed by five layers. Each layer represents one of the five groups of Alpha power words. The top layer, or apex, of the pyramid is home to the most powerful group and the bottom layer represents the least powerful words of the five groups.

1. The first group, called the *Direct Power Pattern*, has the most powerful words.

There are only three words that reside within this layer. The three power words are:

* Yes
* Now
* Stop

The strongest word within this group is also the most powerful word in the world. That word is "YES." When you want someone to do something and they say "YES," your mission is complete.

When you have your future partner saying "YES," he is in a positive mindset.

Think back to the episode of driving in San Diego on a perfect day and pulling into the classic car lot. The "salesman" asked you three questions to which you replied to all three with a "YES." He just programmed your mind into the positive mindset he wanted you to have so you would continue to move forward and purchase the car. It worked, didn't it?

"YES," affirms something someone said and it seals the deal.

Have you ever notice that people who are in charge usually give short answers? Did you just say, "YES?" Ah ha, you must be in charge. YES does make you powerful. How do you feel NOW?

NOW is a powerful word and it is easy to place into sentences that usually do not have the NOW. When you place the word in the sentence, it will change the time element of taking action. Here is a good example; when would NOW be a good time to start learning these words and phrases?

We have all lived with and obeyed the simple word STOP. The simple illustration and most common one is the STOP sign we see while we drive. YES, we make a full STOP NOW or we could pay the legal consequence of disobeying the STOP sign.

2. The second layer is called the *Consequential Power Pattern* group.

The word in this group is:

* Because

This word implies there is a consequence associated with something.

Because you failed to call, I didn't meet you for our game.

Because the sun came up, the morning got light.

Because your widget failed, we will replace it at no charge.

The word AND is used as a consequential modifier. You may have more than one AND in the same sentence. Because you were prepared, we got the sale AND you got promoted AND you got a pay raise.

Because you are reading this, you want to learn the material AND start using the information AND start earning more money from helping more people.

3. The third layer is called the *Expansive Power Pattern* group.

The two key words in this group are:

* Beyond
* Expand

Expansive Power Patterns help people see Beyond where they are now and how they can Expand their horizons of unlimited possibilities. An example is: I can tell that ABC company can see BEYOND tomorrow and you can see how by using my product, you are going to EXPAND your sales force and set new sales records.

This is all about the future and the possibilities within the future.

4. Our fourth layer is called the *Sequential Power Pattern*.

The words in this group are:

* Before
* While
* After

This is a concept of things happening in a certain order:

* Before something happens
* While something happens
* After something happens

This is a NATURAL progression of not knowing something BEFORE you learned that knowledge and gaining information WHILE you were learning and finally AFTER you learned the knowledge you are more powerful.

Here are two examples:

* BEFORE you read about conversational hypnosis, you didn't have the tools you are availing yourself of NOW. WHILE you are reading this book, and AFTER you finish this book, you are going to be more powerful with your verbal skills and help more people get what they want.
* BEFORE you heard of the ABC Widget Company, you probably thought "HOW am I going to solve this problem?" WHILE you listened to me speak and described it's benefits, you started to see possibilities. BECAUSE of it's possibilities AND AFTER you start using your widget, you are going to feel relieved that the solution is finally here where you know it should be.

5. The fifth layer is called the *Experiential Power Pattern*.

The words in this group are:

* Realize
* Aware

This power pattern of words draws attention to the obvious.

If you are in your office, you are AWARE of items in the office and you do not REALIZE all the items in your office.

Your friend, Chris, walks into your room and he wants you to tell him everything in the office that starts with the letter C. You never thought about that before, yet you are AWARE of items in the room that start with the letter C. You begin to REALIZE there are more items that start with the letter C than you expected.

The most obvious one would be Chris since he made the request (did you think of him)? You start your list of Chris, clock, cash, coin, computer, coffee cup etc. YES, you were AWARE those items were in your room AND you did not REALIZE there were that many items in your room.

When you use these words properly, you are taking something that is not necessary factual and making it factual. Here is an example:

* I am certain that you REALIZE ABC Widgets are the best widgets in the industry AND you are AWARE of the potential this company has for growth with endless possibilities.

You are taking something in the example that is not necessarily factual and making it factual. You are painting their experience as if they have experienced it in the past or you are making it so obvious that the statement has to be true.

These words within the five groups are called POWER WORDS make people do what you want them to do. As stated earlier in the book, you have all this information stored in your brain.

You have used these words all your life BUT the big question you need to ask yourself is this: "Have I been using these words in the proper order?" I think we both know the answer to that question.

There are a multitude of words that can be made from the 26 letters of the alphabet. This is your lucky day because you only have to work on eleven (11) words that you already know and use daily. You REALIZE you use these words everyday and NOW you are AWARE that you must use them in the proper order.

BEFORE you start using the proper format, you must learn the format AND WHILE you learn the format you need to practice, practice and practice AND don't STOP.

AFTER you are proficient with the format you will REALIZE the tremendous benefits BEYOND your goals AND you will EXPAND your goals.

BECAUSE you are NOW a solution specialist, you are AWARE of the solution needed for your future partners AND they will say YES to your solution. Congratulations, you have done your work perfectly!

This was all accomplished while you had your future partners in the light stage of hypnosis called the Alpha stage or waking stage of hypnosis. You are NOW in an elite group of $ucce$$ful people that use hypnosis daily.

Hypnosis is used daily in many arenas, from the medical field to the political field and many in between the two.

Below is a diagram of the pyramid. Please use it as your personal study guide AND as a flow chart of Power Patterns. There is room on the pyramid for you to fill in the proper words for each power pattern layer.

This is a section that you will want to come to and read and reread several times. This is also a good section to come to on a regular basis for your recurrent training. It will reinforce your persuasive power pack vocabulary that will allow you to create the appropriate solution for your future partners.

Good luck and hang on because you are going to have a tremendous ride!

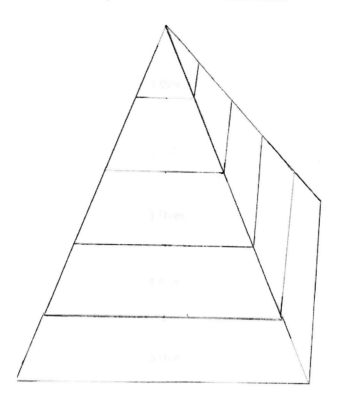

Name the 5 levels of Power Patterns

1. _____

2. _____

3. _____

4. _____

5. _____

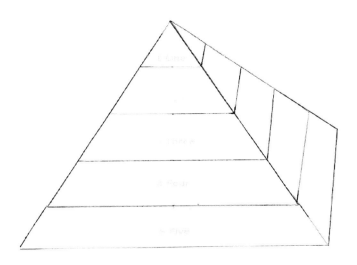

1. DIRECT POWER PATTERN

2. CONSEQUENTIAL POWER PATTERN

3. EXPANSIVE POWER PATTERN

4. SEQUENTIAL POWER PATTERN

5. EXPERIENTIAL POWER PATTERN

DISCOVER THE POWER OF EMBEDDED COMMANDS

Many people are AWARE of embedded commands and REALIZE they should be using them to improve their $ucce$$.

The reason they are not using embedded commands is BECAUSE no one has ever taken the time to fully explain their benefits AND how to use them. After they learn the process of using embedded commands, studies have shown their closing rate goes BEYOND what it is at the present time and their business will EXPAND. BEFORE you start using embedded commands with your future partners, you must practice. WHILE you practice, you will discover it is becoming easier and easier to use the commands and AFTER you are proficient using embedded commands, you will have another powerful tool for your tool box.

Embedded commands are used to get someone to do something you want them to do. You will embed words within your vocabulary that will cause someone to do something you want them to do and yet, it has nothing to do with the subject matter of the message.

Within your message, you will break down your embedded command to three words. Have you noticed the string of threes throughout this book?

You can use embedded commands when you are having a conversation with someone face to face or on the phone. Yes, you can use embedded commands in written print, email and even in text messaging AND we will discuss each one.

Another name for embedded commands is analog marking. Clear as mud, right?

Analog marking means you are going to mark out some words in a phrase or sentence and reduce the words to three words for someone to do something you command. This is part of conversational hypnosis, which means you do not need to have anyone in a deep trance.

Since you are talking with someone, you have many more options, meaning you can use gestures and techniques when you are eyeball to eyeball. Some examples would be touching your ear, talking a little louder, tapping on something, taking a step or anything else you can think of when you get to the "three words."

When you do something different getting to each of the three words, those three words will stand out in the recipient's subconscious mind. When you do your embedded commands properly, you have around an 80% success rate of having the person do what you want he or she to do.

You may be asking yourself how this works with the written word. You will be happy and surprised to learn the subconscious mind interprets written words as if they were spoken. That means your written words will be transformed into an audio format in your subconscious mind. Amazing, isn't it?

Here is an example that will be used to embed a command:

"While I was walking down the street, a car went by. I noticed a Scratch on it and I wondered if it was Your car. I said to myself, I wonder if he Knows about the scratch?"

The command to you is to "scratch your nose." Therefore, in the example we have several options to use to relay the command.

The words in the example for the command are *scratch, your* and *knows*. When a person gets to each of the three words, he can raise his voice slightly, speak a little louder or use the same gesture at each of the three words.

A gesture could be something as subtle as pulling on your ear, rubbing your elbow, tapping on something, taking a step forward or backward, coughing, a facial expression or any other gesture you want. However, you must do the same subtle gesture for all three words.

You probably noticed in the example the word "knows" and what we want our person to scratch is his "nose." Two different words. However, remember from above we learn that the subconscious mind processes information only in the audio format.

Since "knows" and "nose" sound alike, the spelling has no bearing at all. This process is known as "Dhonological Ambiquity" and no you do not need to memorize that. There is no test on this.

If you have processed this, NOW is the time to move on and answer what you are NOW thinking. What happens when we don't talk to someone face-to-face?

Obviously our options are not as vast and the format is basically the same.

How do we put in the embedded command or secret message in a text format? Let's use the same example and text that message to someone.

When you get to the "words," capitalize the first letter of each of the three "words" in the message. You can capitalize all the letters of the three words but that may allow your receiver to catch on to your trick and now you are busted.

If your phone has the capability of changing the font style, size, italic, underline or color you can use any of these options.

When writing a letter or composing one with your computer, you can use the same options as above plus change the writing style for the three words. You also have the **BOLD** option on your computer to use.

Emailing is the same as above. Be careful not to go to extremes because you will get caught and your message is no longer your secret message or the embedded command.

There are ways to relay your command while you are talking on the phone.

When you get to each of the three words, you can press a key button to create a tone, tap on the phone's microphone, have music playing in the background and adjust the volume at the beginning of each word or anything else you can think of that will be different while you are talking. Probably the easiest method is to speak slightly louder when you get to each of the three words.

You need to practice this procedure on your friends and don't let them know you are doing this experiment. If they catch on, they just told you that you need more practice.

Once you feel like you are getting proficient, go to a party and try your skills on ten people at the party. The reason to use ten people is because it is an easy way to determine your percentage of success.

Prior to the party, write a script of what you are going to say with your embedded command. Be sure it is a command that will have the people perform the command while you are at the party. This way you will have a way to test your progress. When you get a rate of 80% or higher, you are ready to use embedded commands on your future partners.

4 SIMPLE STEPS FOR CLOSING

We think in two different awareness levels; conscious and sub-conscious levels.

Our conscious level is our "critical factor" or logical factor. It determines that what we hear or say is reality and the source of all judgments.

Our subconscious level does not know how to make judgments. It is or it isn't, just like a computer.

A persuader uses psychosomatic words and tonality to make an impact on the future partners' subconscious level. That causes the future partners to change the way they think, which causes a change in the way they act.

If you want to have a person change what they do or want, you must first change the way they think.

Aha, you just learned a critical key in persuasion.

But wait, there's more!

So please keep on reading.

The key elements in persuasion are:

* Getting the future partners to trust you thinking you are an authority on your product or service. This is part of rapport.
* Getting your future partners to relax with an open mind and let go of their old beliefs and ideas; also part of rapport.
* Getting your future partners to let go of their critical factors and allow their subconscious mind to accept what you are saying is true, factual and for the good of the future partners.
* Acting "as if." It's thinking in the future and painting a positive picture for your future partners.

Each one of these is an important and powerful element.

You must show your confidence in your product or service and your persuasion. This will allow your future partners to believe in what you are saying when you show a high level of confidence.

Your future partners will think there must be something about your product or service that they don't know. The best part is, they NOW know they "want" your product or service.

Remember IASM? I Am Sold Myself.

Your future partner always has this FM station tuned in: WIIFM.

What's In It For Me?

When your future partner sees and feels your enthusiasm, he will realize that there is something great in it for him. He will become happily involved with your product or service.

You must act "as if" and paint that picture in the future. Explain all the benefits and features you can to fit the future partners' needs, wants and desires. You will have a customer for life.

That's the way you want it, isn't it?

During this process you must always be morally and ethical correct. That allows you to be excited and truthful about your product or service.

When you run your business this way, you will always have new future partners because "good word of mouth" will fill your money bucket.

You become that extraordinary pro that helps people.

What's the difference between ordinary and extraordinary? Just a little extra. Here are some examples of doing a little extra:

* Reframing or changing the frame around the picture of what other salespeople are selling. Your future partners NOW have a different perspective of your product or service.

You plant ethical seeds of doubt about what your future partner thinks or feels about the other person's product or service. You open his mind to your product or service.

You work just like a lawyer in court defending his client. He makes a statement to the jury to plant seeds of doubt.

That phrase is "beyond a shadow of doubt." Remember to use our phrase, "has anyone ever taken the time to FULLY explain ALL the features and benefits of _____?"

Go back and read that phrase again. Do you see any powerful words? Do you see any words that create doubt in your mind? What will that phrase do to your customer's mind?

There are two words in that phrase that you should examine and study. Look at the words "fully" and "all." What is special about these two words?

We will examine the word "fully" first. Ask yourself why is "fully" an important word in the phrase?

Words that end in "ly" are hypnotic words. Why? Because the "ly" allows your mind to fill in the blanks. In this phrase, the blank is what was left out if explanation was not fully explained. There must be something missing and my mind will fill in the missing information.

Study these few sentences and pick out the hypnotic words and what they created.

"You obviously know how to relax, and it is clearly your right and privilege to enjoy relaxation. Apparently, you have been having some stress in your life, and now it is time to let all of that go. Certainly, you know how to day-dream and how to go to sleep at night."

Now pick out the hypnotic words. If you found three, you have not found all of the words. If you found five, you are guessing. Congratulations, you picked out four hypnotic words. You are doing perfectly. What are the four words? They are:

* Obviously
* Clearly
* Apparently
* Certainly

Obviously is a word that leaves out what is obvious. Clearly is missing information compared to what? Apparently is like clearly as compared to what? Certainly falls into the same reasoning, compared to what?

Your mind has to work and fill in the blanks for all of the "ly" words. That allows your future partner to paint the picture in his mind of whatever he wants to paint.

The second word in the phase that is "ALL." This plants the seeds of doubt. The future partner will think the other companies may NOT have explained ALL of the features and benefits. If the other companies did not explain ALL, then what else are they NOT telling the customer?

A powerful technique you should learn and use is the use of mind triggers.

Mind triggers are telling your future partner while he is doing something later today or tomorrow, he will be thinking of what you tell them to think about.

This is a subtle tactic that works extremely well.

An example of this is:

You are showing a home to a couple. The home you show them is exactly what they wanted except for the investment.

They wanted a home with a large amount of square footage to accommodate their growing family.

As you walk them through the home you say, notice how roomy your home feels and how your family can adapt to this home easily.

This is the size of home you said you needed and wanted, isn't that right?

Later today, as you drive back home you will realize how this home is the home you want and all of the other small, cramped homes just would not fit your criteria. This is the mind trigger.

You can NOW realize a mind trigger is a form of hypnosis.

As you continue to read this book, you can find other forms of hypnosis. In fact, you have already read other forms of hypnosis and did not realize they were hypnosis.

You are in a different mindset and your mind is NOW more open to the possibilities of tonality with your words.

You will NOW have a stronger desire to learn different closing techniques that will propel your sales to a different height.

That last line was a SEED planted in your subconscious mind. Said in different words, hypnosis was performed on you.

If you are still reading this book, I know what type of person you are.

You do want to learn and apply new skills, procedures and methods to close more sales, right? Of course you do, otherwise you would have closed this book long ago.

When you discover and apply just one golden nugget to your persuasion, you will gain more:

* Self esteem
* Belief
* Confidence

* Skill
* Knowledge
* and, of course, MONEY

Once you have accomplished this, then all my work, effort, time and commitment to write this book will be worthwhile.

I want to help you succeed.

I DARE YOU TO USE THESE HYPNOTIC SELLING SECRETS AND NOT DRAMATICALLY INCREASE YOUR TRAFFIC, YOUR SALES AND YOUR BUSINESS. . .
100% GUARANTEED!

By now you realize that traditional selling uses the form of presentation and very little, if any, persuasion. That is a main reason why so many salespeople fail in the arena of sales.

The salesman knows and expects a sale at the end of his presentation. If he receives an objection or resistance to the offer, he does not know how to close.

The average salesman knows about three closing techniques. Studies have shown that most sales require approximately seven closes before the sale is made.

True, the closes are made throughout the presentation and that means there should not be any resistance to the sale at the end of the presentation. This sounds good on paper and that did work in the past. Today, however, today we have a different story.

You have learned that today you must be a solution specialist and help people discover the solution to their problem, want or need. We get to that point by asking questions.

Asking the right question at the proper time is the most powerful tool you will have in your toolbox. You will discover asking questions will out perform the traditional sales closings you learned years ago.

An easy way to measure your results would be to look at your bank account and compare today's bottom line to yesterday's bottom line.

By now you are probably wondering what questions should be asked?

The questions to ask are the ones to discover and uncover the events that created the issues your people have.

If you don't know what caused the pain, how can you heal the pain? Through your conversation of asking questions and listening to the response, both you and your people will have a clearer picture of the issue and you will have acquired the information needed to formulate the customized solution to the issue.

Do not share the solution at this point in time. You need to ask questions to find out if your people are really aware of the fact they have an issue and if they want to do something to resolve their issue.

Ask them if their issue has been affecting them and what they have tried to get rid of the issue. If they did try to resolve their issue and did not succeed, ask them how that made them feel.

Listen to their response and ask if it is important at this time to have their issue eliminated. If they say no, it's time for you to go.

If they say YES, ask how they would feel by no longer having that issue and what would that mean for them. When you ask these factual and feeling questions, you learn if there is an issue and they have a desire to solve that issue. You then know if you have a solution that will take care of their need.

At this stage, you are not concentrating on a sale; you are discovering if there is a sale to be made. Build your questions around what is happening at the present time and how that has changed their lives.

Ask if they would like to go back to the time prior to having their issue. Ask how that would benefit them and how that would make them feel.

Once they answer your questions, ask if they are ready to make a change to have the same life style prior to the issue. When they say YES, ask what they feel like they need to do to get rid of their issue.

By asking these types of questions, you are getting your people to share what they think and feel would be the correct procedure to solve their issue. When you ask these questions, your future partners' subconscious will realize the value of who you are and the value of your offer even before you offer your solution.

When your people verbalize their solution, they become part of the process and it makes them feel like they want and must take action. Once they are at this point in your persuasion, you don't have to do anything externally to motivate their action.

Asking questions put you in control and pushes the conversation in the right direction. It paints a picture in the peoples' mind, allowing you to see their picture through their words.

If their picture is not complete, you know what questions to ask to have them complete their picture. Ask what they would do, if they could, that would complete their picture. Be prepared to get answers like these:

* I could never do that.
* That's just a pipe dream.
* I gave up on that a long time ago.

When you get comments like these, you then ask:

What if you could do something and there was nothing stopping you?

Listen very carefully to their response because you will hear their real desires because you have built rapport and they trust you. Their answers will give them a broader view of what can be for them.

Give them time for their subconscious mind to process what they just said. They now realize they can make a change to better their lifestyle. Ask questions to ensure they are on the same path as you. Once you know they are ready for change you ask this:

"What if you took this approach (share your solution.)? Would that make it easier for you?"

You don't tell them what you know; you ask questions that allow them to discover what you know. That gives your people the feeling that they own the solution. That's the way you want it, isn't it?

For those of you that have been in sales for any length of time, you know that this form of natural selling is different from the traditional selling methods. You may feel overwhelmed at this point in time and feel like there is a lot of information and techniques to learn.

Don't worry, it just takes practice and it won't be long before you will feel comfortable using your new skills in getting people happily involved with your product or service.

THE REAL TRUTH ABOUT PERSUASION EQUATION

The persuasion equation is a step-by-step process that gets people to shift from where they are to a new belief structure. By Marshall Sylver The steps are:

Rapport is paramount: You must believe in your product or service to be able to market it to the public.

To be believable in your product you need to own your product. Then and only then can you describe it with feelings and paint the picture for your future partners with feelings.

Remember, emotions sell and logic locks in the sale.

Elicit your future partners outcome.

How do we do that?

This is done by our words, tonality and body language.

Our words make up approximately 7-10% of our communication.

Tonality makes up to 30-35% when we are speaking one on one and about 70% when we are on the phone.

Our body language makes up about 60% when we are face to face with our future partners.

You may be asking yourself if the 7-10% is correct, so let me explain. Words are very important, because without them, we would have a tough time communicating.

Words have a low percentage because it is the tonality of those words that make the impact. Here is an example:

The dog bit Rick. Rick bit the dog. The same four words were used in each sentence; however, the order or tonality of the words made a totally different story.

- Help your future partners get happily involved with your product or service. Have your persuasion message perfected and have all the doors closed prior to the close so the future partners' decision to say YES is easy for them.
- Give more information if you get resistance.

Resistance is the future partners' way of asking for more information. With the new information, they can use logic, the critical mind, to solidify their emotional minds of getting happily involved with your product or service.

- You NOW need to close again and again and again. Most closes will require at least three tries before your future partners say YES. Of course, you try mini closes during the persuasion so when you get to the close, it should be easy.

Sales is a game of communication.

You must rehearse, review and revise to achieve the level of being a professional.

It is your responsibility to help people get happily involved with your product or service. The amount of money you earn is a yardstick of the service you give to your future partners. More service gives more money.

Since words are so important in communication, there are some words we should NOT use in our communication.

We shouldn't use words that will have a negative affect on your persuasion capabilities or at least have a less than desirable affect on your persuasion.

These words are not in any specific order and no word is more or less harmful than the other. Here are words you should take out of your persuasion vocabulary:

* TRY: Think about this for awhile.

How can anybody try? Either you do or you don't!

Try is poor because it implies failure or a C.Y.A. (cover your assets) or an out for you.

If you meet a friend and that friend says let's have lunch tomorrow and you say, sounds good, I'll try. Tomorrow arrives, (yes, I know tomorrow never arrives), your friend is at the restaurant waiting for you and you never show.

In your friend's mind you lied to him because you did not hold up your end of the plan. Later that afternoon your friend calls and asks why you never showed up for lunch and you say, "I tried."

Let's bring this down to the basics of goal setting.

You set your goals for the year and one of your goals is to make a million dollars by the end of the year. The end of the year is here and you do not have a million dollars and you say, "I tried."

You gave yourself that out for failure, didn't you? You must say I am going to earn a million dollars by the end of the year. You create a plan broken down into steps to be achieved during the year to reach your goal by year's end. Plan your work and work your plan.

NOW, I want you to say "I remove the word "try" from my vocabulary." Guess what? You have just programmed your subconscious mind to remove "try."

* CAN'T. Can't never did anything! Remove it NOW.

Have you ever asked someone to do something for you and they responded by saying, I can't?

What did they really mean?

Did you ask them what they meant by saying I can't?

Probably not.

Whenever someone tells you "I can't," you should ask them this: "When you say 'I can't,' do you mean you don't know *how* to or you don't want to?"

If they say they don't know how to, you NOW have information you can use to continue. They can learn how to do what you wanted them to do.

If they say they don't want to, you ask them, "What is it that you want?" and move on from there.

If they don't know what they want and have no interest at all, they are a suspect and stealing your time.

Some people will actually lie to you when that happens. They are nothing more than weak suspects and not your niche.

There is a phrase that applies to this: Some will. Some won't. So what NEXT?

NOW, I want you to say "I remove the word "can't" from my vocabulary." Yep, you have just programmed your subconscious mind to remove "can't" from your vocabulary.

Probably you NOW know when you program your mind, you are actually doing self-hypnosis.

* BUT, is the next word to take out of your vocabulary.

You may have a big BUT in your life, which keeps you from getting what you want.

Your BUT negates everything prior to it. Here are some examples.

I want to be successful, but it takes a lot of work.

I want to be healthier, but it means eating right and working out.

Any place you use BUT you need to replace your BUT with AND. Get the BUT out of there. By replacing your BUT with AND, you will change your mindset on everything.

NOW, I want you to say, "I remove the word BUT from my vocabulary."

You have just programmed your subconscious mind to remove BUT from your vocabulary.

Going back to the first BUT sentence, read it with AND.

I want to be successful AND I know it will take a lot of work.

The second sentence.

I want to be healthier AND it means eating right and working out.

Notice the difference. We went from a negative to a positive in our writing and it created a different mindset.

We will place this into a close and see the improvement when you read the change.

Let's go to an example of marketing water conditioners to a homeowner.

You get to the close and they say, "It sounds good BUT we are going to look around." You say, "Oh, I agree with you because you want to check around AND make sure you are getting a quality piece of equipment that will fulfill your needs, wants and desires, don't you?" They say, "YES."

What they are really saying is, "We need more information." The next thing to say is, "What is it about this water conditioner that did not fulfill your needs, wants and desires?"

After they tell you the reason for not buying, you NOW have more information and will revise and go back into the close.

These are three major words to remove from your vocabulary:

TRY, CAN'T and BUT.

In a moment, you will be given three more words that are spineless words. These words are wishy-washy words and they don't really carry much validity. The first word is:

* HOPE, as in I hope I will win the lottery.

Good luck with that one! I hope my business improves. I hope I do well in school.

We all want to do business with people that KNOW what they are doing instead of HOPING to be able to do what you want.

If you had to get some legal advise from a lawyer, you would go to his office and he says I "hope" what I can do will help, you should turn around and run out of his office. What you want to hear is I "know" what I need to do to help you, don't you?

* IF I tell you the next word, will you get it?

When I tell you the next word, you will get it.

Have you found the word yet?

The word is "IF."

It is a spineless wimpy word, right? It is a word that leaves us an out.

Yes, I know that "LIFE" is half "IF" and too many people use the middle two letters in life as their scapegoat. Don't be one of those people. More examples.

If I can find the house of your dreams.

If I can get you the sports car you want.

It promises nothing and there is no importance in an IF sentence.

Replace that IF with WHEN and hear the difference.

When I find the house of your dreams and WHEN I get the sports car you want. Everything sounds much better, right?

Please answer this question:

Do you want any more problems in your life?

Of course not and yet you do like to be challenged, don't you?

People don't mind challenges and they hate problems.

When a partner calls and says I have a problem with your service you respond by asking what is the "challenge" you are having?

Saying that, you have just changed the mindset of your partner and you are his friend that is going to help. It does PAY to be a friend.

You do want money and become financially free, don't you?

By applying these principles throughout the book, you can improve your lifestyle and create a better life for your family.

Yes, some of the techniques explained may sound strange to you. You will feel uncomfortable changing your habits when you start to apply your new techniques.

Just ask yourself this question:

Is it worth it to learn a new and better way to perform in my arena to get more positive results?

In two to three months from now you will be amazed of the easy transition it was to become more successful and richer.

To help you through this process, get a vision board and put pictures of what you want on the vision board.

Look at your vision board daily and that will reinforce your goals. It will help you achieve what it is you want, need or desire.

When you become more focused, the time to reach your goals will be shorter and you will reap the benefits of your labor sooner. That is what you want, isn't it?

Then just DO IT!!!!

MONKEY SEE, MONKEY DO MIRRORING AND MATCHING

When you are talking with your future partners face to face, you have a huge benefit that is not enjoyed through the internet or over the phone.

That benefit is, you are able to mirror and match your future partners.

When you mirror, do it properly. Remember when looking into a mirror, images are reversed. Why is that important?

When you comb your hair, brush your teeth or just look into a mirror, you see yourself reversed of what you are doing. You brush your teeth using your right hand and the other person in the mirror, your image, is using the left hand.

What does this mean for you? When you are talking with your future partner and he scratches his head using his right hand, you need to scratch your head using your left hand. That is the mirror effect.

Don't try to mirror all movements as they happen. Be shrewd so you don't come across as a mime.

Be careful not to let them realize you are using that tactic because a tactic known is a sale blown.

You want to gain rapport with your future partners because they will not buy from you if they don't like or trust you.

We all trust people like ourselves and by matching your future partner's body language, you are sending the message of "I am just like you." Subconsciously, this increases his comfort level and decreases his resistance. You and he are in synch. By adopting the body language of your future partner, you are telling him on a non-verbal level that you and he have something in common.

When you appear to be similar to him, you are more trusted and harder to resist. Studies have proven that people cannot resist themselves or their own actions.

Besides mirroring and matching, you can induce hypnosis with your smile. Your smile sends a message of let's be friends. The next time you are in an elevator and someone gets on after you, look them in the eyes and then give them a big smile. You will see that you will get a big smile in return.

You must set the stage before the play begins. Said in a different way, you must do your steps in the correct order to achieve the proper results.

A person building a house wouldn't build the roof before he had the foundation poured and the walls up, would he?

A cook wouldn't ice a cake before the cake is baked, would she?

The same logic is used with your persuasion.

You don't ask for the close as soon as you meet your future partners.

You first gain rapport, give your persuasion and then do the paperwork. You follow a checklist of things to do in the proper order.

Let's replace the word "checklist" with cash-list because that is exactly what it provides.

To gain rapport, you must emulate your future partners as much as you can because that will make them feel comfortable with you.

Of course a key element in all persuasion is to have eye contact with your future partners.

You say the same words and phrases that they use and you speak in the same tone, volume and speed as the future partners do.

Always set the stage before the play.

This phrase works extremely well for those of you in outside sales.

Below is a procedure that works extremely well when you are in the customer's environment.

When you get to the front door, knock and do not ring the doorbell.

Why? Friends knock. Strangers use the doorbell.

This is your first step in creating rapport with your customer.

When the homeowners open the door, be about four feet back from the door. Walk up to the door after it is opened.

This step is two-fold:

If the couple has a peek hole in the door and they look through to see who is knocking, they see you are away from the door and not a threat.

The other reason is after the door is opened you slowly walk to the door just like a friend would do.

When you get to the door,

introduce yourself, with a firm handshake.

State who you work for and continue with,

"I'm a couple of minutes early for our appointment."

This tells the homeowner that you respect his time as being valuable and you are punctual.

As you walk into the home say:

- It's a great day, isn't it? They say YES
- If there is a nice painting on the wall, say while you are pointing to the painting, I see you enjoy the finer things in life, don't you? they say YES
- If they have a dog, say we have dogs also and I know your dog is one of the family members, right? and YES

Did you realize you got "the three questions" asked to get all YES answers? This gets the homeowner's mindset into a positive mode; very important tactic and you have taken control.

As you go into the living room, comment on how beautiful their home looks.

Ask how old their home is.

After they answer, say, "So this is your HOME HOME then, right?

The reason for this is if you are selling an item for the home, you want to be sure they are planning to live there for years and have no plans to move in the near future.

You are closing doors as soon as you can.

Plan for the close before you get into the home.

Conduct some small talk such as:

- How long have you lived here?
- Where did you live before?
- How did you come to settle in this area?
- Was it easy to find this home?
- How many houses did you look at before you knew this was the home?
- What did you like best about this home?
- What types of improvements have you made to your home?
- What improvements are going to be made in the future?
- How soon will those improvements take place?

* What is your next improvement going to be?
* When are you planning to do that?
* What was your reason for me to be here today?
* Is getting (your product) important to you?
* When do you plan on getting (the product?)
* I commend you on wanting to get (the product) and I can share with you that you will be very happy with (the product). I have (the product) in my home and we NOW REALIZE we should have done this years ago because it has saved us a ton of money and we enjoy the benefits of being comfortable because the (product) is priceless! You're going to love (the product) as much as we love ours.

This line of questioning takes them back in time and gives you the information of how they got to where they are today. They told you what their pain is and it allows you the mental cashlist to follow and suggest your solution to their pain.

You gathered their information while you were in the living room where the family entertains their guest and get to know people. Now is the time to suggest you need some space to share information with them and the best place to do that is at the kitchen table so let's please move in there.

NOW stand up and start walking towards the kitchen.

This is a major point.

You want to get out of the living room where the kids are watching TV.

You want to be in the kitchen where you become a member of the family. Not a stranger.

The real family bonding takes place in the kitchen.

Tell the homeowners where to sit and that is another major point.

If you are a male, have the husband sitting next to you and his wife next to him. The reason for this is twofold.

You want the husband and wife sitting next to each other so you can see both of them at the same time.

Many salesmen lose sales when the husband and wife sit at opposite sides of the table and the salesman is sitting between the two.

When the salesman is looking at the wife for approval of the sale, the husband is giving hand gestures to the wife of no purchase and vice versa.

The other major reason of that sitting arrangement is this. You do not want any doubt from the husband of you touching his wife.

Ladies, when you are in the home, be sure you have the wife next to you and the husband next to his wife for the same reasoning.

Make sure there is NO sexual innuendo at all.

In this example, let's assume you are marketing water conditioners.

Now is the time to find their WHY to the water conditioner. You ask, Mr. and Mrs., Homeowner, in the living room you stated that you wanted a water conditioner. My question is WHY do you want a water conditioner?

Now shut up and let them tell you WHY.

They may say things like the water tastes bad, smells bad, and leaves stains on their fixtures and water spots on the car after it is washed. They are buying bottled water and they hate the hassle and expense.

Once they have shared the reasons for why they want the water conditioner, you say something like this:

"How does that make you feel having all of those issues with your present water supply?"

You keep on asking questions like: "What have you done in the past to get rid of those issues?"

"Did any of those procedures get rid of your water issues?"

"By now, you realize you need to find a solution to your issues, don't you?"

"If there is a way to get rid of your issues with the water and provide good wholesome tasting water that is good for your health, you would be interested in that, wouldn't you?

"How would you feel and what benefits would you realize by having that quality system for your family?"

Shut up and get their responses.

After they have responded, you say this:

"By now, you want to start enjoying those benefits you mentioned for your family, right?"

"Mr. and Mrs. Homeowner, I may know of a solution that will do exactly what you said you wanted."

Shut up and have them ask you for the solution. This NOW puts all the pressure on them and they NOW become the salesmen selling themselves on the solution and they don't even know what the solution is. At this point in time, you are no longer the salesman. Instead, you are their "Doctor of Water" and you are going to get rid of their pain by giving them your prescription.

When they asked you to share your solution, they gave you permission to start your persuasion for their prescription.

Always start your persuasion with this phrase:

"Has anyone ever taken the time to help you FULLY understand ALL the benefits of (fill in the blank with your product or service)?" by Marshall Sylver

This statement is a powerful statement.

It lets the homeowner realize you know your product and will explain ALL the benefits.

It plants seeds of doubt in the couple's minds that the other salespeople didn't know ALL the benefits or didn't want to take time and explain ALL the benefits.

You have just knocked out your competition.

Your future partners now realize you are a professional. You are working for their best interest to fulfill their needs, wants and desires.

After that question get their response and always ask for a **drink of water.**

This "zinger" is another major point in the game of persuasion.

You may not be thirsty so why ask for water? Remember, they have bottled water.

Asking for water gets the homeowner involved and tells you they are on your side. You are NOW more like a family member because they served you.

Remember, you are closing doors all the time. Your persuasion is closing doors continuously before you get to the close.

You have closed several doors already and there was no "selling" or manipulating. Closing doors and programming the mindset!

Make this statement:

In a moment I will share with you what a quality whole house water conditioner can do for you and your family.

Now is the time to animate the water conditioner into a third person.

Explain the benefits by stating "that little guy is going to be working for you night and day,"

- 24 hours a day
- 7 days a week
- and 365 days a year

Yes, he does have a big job ahead of him. The best part is he loves doing his work,

- never complains
- never asks for a payment or allowance

* never talks back
* and is always there at your beckoning command.

Oh, if only our kids could be half that efficient.

He is going to provide you with the best tasting water you've ever had or will have in this home starting today and continue on into the future, just the way you want it, isn't it?

Not only that, he is going to save you money on laundry supplies,

* have your dishes come cleaner in the dishwasher,
* have your car clean without those nasty water spots
* and clean your entire water system from the buildup of elements collecting inside your plumbing pipes.

This little guy is going to make you feel better about yourself.

You NOW will enjoy that clean, fresh and great tasting water that is better for your health than drinking that chlorine based water from your tap.

You will also discover that he is going to give your skin a treat.

Once you take a bath or shower with his water you will feel the softness of your skin. That softness is actually your own natural oils on your skin that were always stripped away from your old water system.

Isn't natural good? (Nod your head up and down when you ask that question so they will agree with you)

Not only will your skin thank you, your plants will thank you because they too will be drinking pure water.

Water, just like the kind God created for us.

You will see how well the plants thrive after they become happily involved with your new water system.

By now, you realize this little guy is going to be working for you around the clock and providing more benefits than you ever thought of, isn't that true?

Plant many seeds into the homeowner's minds of how their life-style will improve by having their "little guy" in their home as quickly as possible.

Explain the benefits their newest member of the family will do for them and ask each person what they want to experience most with their new water system.

After they have shared what they want the most of all the benefits, YOU NOW know their "hot buttons" to push to close for the sale.

Sell benefits, sell benefits and sell benefits.

Some of you may feel this is too pushy and this is going for the jugular vein. If you do, then you have not yet changed your mindset.

Shame on you!

Aren't you in the business to help people?

If you are in the business of helping people, aren't you morally and ethically obligated to get people happily involved with a product that will benefit your customer?

If you do not do all you can to get the sale, which will then allow your customer to gain all of the benefits you have with your product, you are doing a disservice to your customer and you need to get out of the persuasion arena.

Near the end of the persuasion, throw in this zinger to get the homeowner off guard and not sound like a "salesman."

By asking this question it is like you are slapping them in the face and they usually will give you an honest answer.

Ask this:

Mr. Homeowner, on a scale of 1 to 10 and 10 being the best, where do I fall?

When they answer, it will normally be an 8 or 9, so ask, "What do I have to do to get it to a 10?"

Most of the time they will state what you need to do to earn the 10. That gives you more information for the close.

They may respond with I don't know.

They say that because they don't want to look as though they didn't understand what you said. Or they may feel like their question isn't that important.

Put them at ease by saying this:

I know you don't know, if you did know, what would it be?

This NOW gives them permission to share their information with you.

Yes, you should use the "if" word here as the wimpy word. Do that to let the customer know you have softened up. At least in their mind you have and you will also be soft at the close.

Ha ha. Not going to happen! You are a PRO!

Many times when the customer feels you have softened a little, he will expose the real reason of not taking action. That new information gives you what you need to close the sale.

In every persuasion there is always a winner and YOU decide who the winner is going to be. It had better be YOU, correct?

Time to rewind. Two huge doors were closed prior to the close. Please do not miss them.

You asked what was the most important benefit each person wanted from the newest member of the family.

You also asked, "What do I NOW need to do to get my score to a 10?"

Folks, these are two awesome, major key players for the close.

You must find their hot buttons, or benefits they want.

You must find what you missed in your persuasion to earn your score of 10.

These two key elements are near the end of your mental checklist (cash-list) of closing sales.

Your cash-list cannot be complete unless you get the answers to those two key questions.

Have you ever put a jigsaw puzzle together and had two missing pieces? The puzzle was not complete.

This is the same.

Your mental sales puzzle is not complete with these two missing elements.

If you do not do this, you will have some resistance at the close. This will be handled later.

You assume the close because you have closed all the doors and there are no unanswered questions, congrats, you have done your job perfectly!

You have only one more question to ask at this point in time and that is:

"Mr. and Mrs. Homeowner the only other information I need is:

- how soon do you NOW WANT to start enjoying ALL of the benefits by getting happily involved with your newest member of your family?"

Now is the time for you to SHUT UP.

Yes, time stands still at this point of the process. Believe me when I say SHUT UP!

Once they say they are ready to take action, continue to close by saying something cute like this:

"Great, all we need to do now is to fill out the adoption papers and schedule for your delivery date.

You are going to love your new family member. Congratulations!"

Start filling out the paperwork and schedule a time for delivery that fits the homeowner's schedule.

Once the paperwork is completed, now is the time for you to ask for their help. Here is what you ask:

"Mr. and Mrs. Homeowner, you are going to be so happy and proud of your new family member that you are going to tell everyone about him.

Who are the first three families you are going to share your good fortune with?"

Write down the names of the families and say:

"You are good friends with the families and you have the same interests, don't you?

I'm sure they would like to have the same benefits as you NOW have with your new family member.

It would be an honor to help your friends on your behalf to take advantage of the product. All I need is their contact number and I will help them for you. Fair enough?

In fact, once your friends become happily involved with their system, your investment will be less. I will give you $100.00 (whatever amount you want to give) as a gift for every customer I gain from your recommendation."

This method will keep your lifeblood flowing in the sales arena.

Let's go back to the point of closing where you were told to SHUT UP!

If you are NEW to the persuasion arena or feel like time will never start, use this trial close:

"Mr. and Mrs. Homeowner, my Mama told me that silence gives consent, I know she was telling me the truth." Immediately extend your hand, shake hands with the homeowner and say:

"You are going to love your new family member. Congratulations!"

After the homeowners have completed the paperwork, you ask for referrals as explained above.

Persuasion is a game of minds and emotions so have fun with it.

Oh, theatrics are involved within the arena and that will be addressed later.

If you think this is somewhat hokey and corny, then get over it.

Your creditors will not ask if you earned your money by being hokey or corny, they will just take your money.

After all, money is the yardstick measurement of service you provide for your customer. I know you want a long stick.

Money is a tool for you to have a better lifestyle for you and your family. You do deserve a better lifestyle, right?

Now I want you to go back and reread the information above about the process of marketing the water conditioner. This time, as you read, find the three places where the sentence starts with the two words of, "By now." You missed them the first time, didn't you? Your subconscious mind did not miss them. Three times, your subconscious mind heard "BUY NOW" instead of "By now" and your mind was programmed in the positive mindset to "BUY NOW" at the close. Use the "By now" wording with your future partners to get them happily involved with your offer. The power of three!

7 STEPS TO OVERCOME RESISTANCE

Of course, if you did a presentation and closed all of the doors during your presentation, you wouldn't have any resistance, would you?

Make sense, right?

I say NO; it makes dollars, and a lot of dollars.

People within the sales arena who know and work their skills are not lacking for money.

These 7 steps are really just common sense things once you get a different mindset and start thinking in a different manner.

That is a book in itself, so let's just get started, shall we?

After you completed your offer or presentation and "IF" you do have resistance or objections, here are some skills to use to overcome the resistance or objections:

1. Welcome the resistance or objection; act as if that is what you expected.

It shows they are interested and need more information.

If they were not, they would have hung up the phone or stopped before you got that far into the presentation.

Savor that moment and learn from it so you will know how to handle it again if it happens.

You need to have situation awareness and respond to the resistance at hand; in fact, you can have fun with this once you have the proper mindset.

2. Really listen.

God gave us two ears and one mouth for a reason.

We should listen twice as much as we speak.

Too many salespeople and people in general are thinking about what they are going to say next while their prospect is talking.

Wrong, wrong, wrong!

If you are thinking about what you are going to say next, how do you know what are the future partners' needs or wants?

Remember, you have something your future partners really need or want, don't you?

Therefore, it is your job to get your future partners happily involved with your offer; otherwise, you are not doing your job.

3. Echo their response back to pull out more information.

Once you do this, they will tell you the real reason they don't want to take action now.

An example of this could be, it costs too much and you say back to them, "Costs too much?"

They will say, "For that price we can't afford it NOW." They have just given you information that you can now use to help them.

What they are saying is, their budget won't fit the investment and they want the product or service.

You now know they need creative financing, so you provide the solution for them.

Remember, your product or service provides benefits for your future partners, and you are obligated to help them get what they want, aren't you?

4. Feed the resistance back to them to qualify them.

Ask them, "In addition to (what the resistance is,) is there any other reason why you would not become happily involved today? Or is that the ONLY reason?"

If there are other reasons or different reasons, this will flush out those other reasons and you now have information to overcome their objections.

5. Overcome the resistance and state why the resistance is unfounded.

If the money is the only reason for your future partners not taking action, you share with them they are probably unaware of all the possible financing products available to help them get what they NOW WANT.

If there was another resistance you learned from "the flush," you handle that resistance and close.

Another way to handle the resistance is to ignore it.

Many times people say NO to find out if you really believe in your product or service.

By ignoring their resistance and moving on, they will probably forget their question; however, if they do ask again, it is an important concern. You must now deal with the resistance and move on with your close.

6. Immediately move to additional benefits of your product or service and recap the benefits you shared before.

Remember to sell the sizzle, not the steak.

Get your future partners to paint a picture in their mind's eye of how they will be better three or four months into the future by your helping them get happily involved with your offer.

7. Believe in your product or service because this is your profession.

Go back to the beginning of this book and read what "enthusiasm" really spells.

The major focus of this information is for you to recognize that as soon as you experience resistance and deal with it, the resistance will fade away.

Since you NOW know how to deal with resistance, and when it comes back during a different persuasion, you will know how to handle it and close.

These are just some of the closes that work well.

There are many others you can use and I will just give you two more for your humor.

I had one sale and I closed the sale in my mind; however, I did not close in the future partners' minds.

When I started the paperwork they said NO.

Picture this:

I am in a suit and tie sitting at the kitchen table and I hear a NO.

That was such a shock to me, which caused me to fall out of the chair and on the floor.

The couple looked at me and started to get out of their chairs to help me up and make sure I didn't hurt myself.

I got up by myself, brushed off my jacket, sat down on the chair, looked at the couple and said,

"Please forgive me, I thought I heard you say NO."

The couple started to laugh. Then I started to laugh, completed the paperwork, and they purchased my product.

Have fun with sales and if you have to, throw in some theatrics.

One more for the road.

I had explained everything to the homeowners and could not get them past the "sleep on it before we make any decision."

I tried every angle I could so the only thing I could do as the last resort was to get their answer in the morning.

If I had to get the answer in the morning, I am not driving back home and then back to their home the next morning.

Naturally, I told them that is not a problem, I will just sleep on the couch and we will talk in the morning.

I got up from the table, went into the living room and sacked out on their couch.

It turned out to be a very short night because they thought for ten minutes and made the decision to become happily involved with my product.

Yes, actions can speak louder than words.

Be bold, be brave, be believable and be you.

We are near the end of the book and yet we are really at the beginning.

Did you notice a combination of many 3's throughout this book?

That was your first introduction in this book to the power of hypnosis persuasion.

You ask three questions to which your future partners have to say YES to all. That gets their minds into a positive mode where they are always saying YES.

When you are at the close, their subconscious mind has been programmed to say YES which tells their conscious mind to say YES.

If you have never persuaded using these methods I beseech you to learn and use these techniques.

Once you have, you will thank me.

AT LAST - AMAZING TELEPHONE CONVERSATION THAT CREATES SALES

This book started by discussing the transition from traditional selling to the method used in the 21st century. Today, we use the form of natural selling or conversational sharing. The majority of the information you learned was directed to speaking with people in person. In addition, we also discussed using the written format and how to get someone's attention, hold their attention and make a decision to get happily involved with your product or service.

Now is the time for us to learn and acquire the skill for speaking to people using the telephone. Yes, we still have telephone solicitors calling today to get our money. Rules and regulations have become more strict, and we are able to have our number on a "do not call" list. That helps keep us from getting calls we do not want.

Telephone "sales calls" are still done today and they are very effective. The twist we have today is usually someone has received an email, a video, or another form of information through the internet. That information aroused his curiosity about a company's product or service. Once a person becomes curious about something, he will want more information. In order for that person to obtain more information, he will provide his name and phone number on an opt-in form and submit that form via the internet.

Since that person wants more information and he provided his phone number, he just gave you permission to call. You are responding to his request, and that is not cold calling.

When you call, you know that he was intrigued with your product or service. We will use an example of starting a home-based business as your product or a possible business opportunity. You know that he could have found you on the internet through Craig's List, Facebook, an ad in the newspapers, flyer, by word of mouth or by a short video.

You will have a format, outline or cashlist to follow while you are talking with your new future partner. You do not have to use the script verbatim; however, you need to stick with the content of the script. Remember, you are not selling. You are having a phone conversation to learn if he has a pain and how you can solve his pain by suggesting a possible solution to his pain. People do not like to be sold and they do like to buy.

When you make your contact call to the person that wanted more information, here is a proven guide for the call:

Connecting Stage: Focus on the other person! You are here to help.

Hi. May I speak to (person's name) please? My name is (your name) and I am calling you because you requested some information on starting a home based business and I am getting back with you to find out how I can help you.

* Can you hear me okay and is this a good time to talk?
* Are you looking for a job or a business?
* Do you know what you are looking for?
* What was it about the ad that attracted your attention?

Revelation Stage: Background Questions. This helps us finding out who the person is and what their background is.

* Are you working now?
* What do you do for a living?
* What made you get involved in that?
* Really, how long have you been doing that?
* (If business) (person's name) you've been doing this for (how many) years, do you like your business?
* (Job) (person's name), you worked for this company for (how many) years, do you like your job?

If answer is YES:

* Why is that? (Say Wow, Um, Right or OK)
* Is there anything that you would change?
* Why would you change that?
* Why is that important to you?

If answer is NO:

* You don't sound very sure….What don't you like about your job/business?
* What do you mean by "Hard Work, Long Hours, Not What You Want To Do?"
* Why do you think you feel that way?
* What type of impact has that had on you?
* In what way?
* (name), is there anything else you don't like about what you do?
* How long has that been going on?
* Would you like to make a change for the better?
* JOB: Besides _____ what is the main reason you are looking for a business other than finding a different type of job?
* BUSINESS: Besides _____ what is the main reason you are looking for another business rather than just focusing on the one you have?

Solution Questions: Getting more insight.

Have you been looking for any other ways to earn money?

What have you been doing about finding something else?

If they have been looking:

- What areas are you looking into?
- Have you looked at anything else? (Say: um, right or OK)
- How did that work out for you?
- What kept you from having success with that?
- What prevented you from starting a business with them?

If they say, "NO," they have not looked at anything

- (Name) what held you back for finding a business?

Set The Stage For Solutions

What about this: What if you could do a business where you would work primarily out of your home?

You would mainly work on your computer and telephone.

Unlike the traditional business, you would not have employees per-se.

You would, however, have people helping you run your business.

For instance, if the business sounds right for you, I will be the person working directly with you.

I will be working with you on a one-on-one basis to make sure you make profit quickly when you start.

I am not, and will not be, your employer or boss.

I will be more like your personal mentor or coach for your success.

Would you be okay with that?

GREAT: Now what about money?

You shared with me you wanted to earn more money, right?

(Name) I have never been in the type of industry you are in.

However, what would you like to earn on an annual basis?

Without any limits, what would you want to earn in a business that you owned?

Let's say they want to earn $150,000 a year

* How close are you to earning that kind of money right now?
* If you stayed where you are today, how many years would it take before you were able to make that kind of money?
* Knowing that, how does that make you feel?
* Let's say we got your income to that point, what would that mean for you?
* How would your life be different from what it is now?
* How would that make you feel?
* In what way?

Consequence Questions:

* (name), I hate to ask you this, because I actually enjoy speaking to you. What are you going to do if nothing changes? If you keep doing what you are doing now, you will not realize any change.
* Are you willing to settle for that?

Qualifying Questions:

* How important is it to you to change your financial situation?
* Is that something you are looking to do now?
* If you could find a business that allows you to have more time with your family and more money, would you be open to an opportunity like that?

The Transition Stage

Opens the door to presenting your solution which is your business opportunity.

Sample Questions:

Based on what you told me, our business might work for you.

With your permission, I would like to briefly go through the details about this business. If you have a pen and paper handy, get them now to take notes.

Presenting Stage

This is a Summary and Agreement. It Demonstrates how the Specific Advantages and Benefits of your Solution (business opportunity) will solve their Pain.

Sample Questions:

* This is what I do and how it would work for you.
* I have a business with a wholesale company called XYZ.
* I work out of my house on my own hours.
* What this means for you is this, if the business does fit you and you are comfortable with me, I will be working with you for the next 90 days.
* I will be doing most of the training with you.
* We'll create a business plan that will allow you to start part-time.
* We will have a goal to replace your income within 90 days.
* After that, you can decide if you want to work your job or if you want to spend more time with your family.

Give a brief overview

* The wholesale company we work for is headquartered in (location)
* We are in the travel business.
* We are part of a discount travel membership.
* Are you familiar with travel discounts?
* If yes, find out more and how are they familiar with travel discount memberships.
* If they say no, share with them that we are like a wholesale travel membership similar to Sam's Club and Costco.

- Here is your next statement: I am going to ask you to visit my website, do you have a pen and paper?
- Give him your website address, tell him it will take about an hour to review everything and ask if he can review the site today.
- If you can, schedule a time to follow up with him tomorrow.

The Carbon Copy

- This is what you will be doing.
- You responded to my ad looking for a business.
- We are going to teach you how to place these types of ads in different parts of the internet, newspapers and magazines.
- This will target people who want to find a business from home and when I get you set up, you'll have about 10 to 15 people a day responding to your ad.
- All you will have to do is to call these people, like I've called you, and ask them some of the same questions I've asked you.
- It's like an interview process.
- If you feel like the business is what they might be looking for, invite them to your website. Your website will educate them.
- Your website will do most of the rest of the work for you.
- Do you feel comfortable doing something like that?
- It's not rocket science.
- I've enjoyed speaking with you (name.)
- Is there anything you would like to address me at this point?
- Great, we will be in touch tomorrow if that is appropriate.

2ⁿᵈ CALL or FOLLOW-UP CALL

The Committing Stage

This is the call that helps the person to commit to the opportunity and start the process of his home based business.

- Hi (name) this is (your name) calling you back.
- Did you make it through the website?
- *If they say NO,* ask them when they will be able to view the website and reschedule another call.

- *If they say YES,* ask what they liked best about what they saw and heard.
- Do you feel like this is a business that will work for you?
- Would you feel comfortable having me be your mentor, coach or trainer?
- I will be the one doing most of the training with you.
- On a scale of 1 to 10.
- 1 being not a business for you.
- 10 being a business that fits your criteria.
- Where do you rate yourself on that scale?

If they say 7 or higher:

- That's pretty high, why so high?
- What do we have to do to get to the 10?

If they say 5 or 6:

- Oh, that's right in the middle, why in the middle?
- What do we have to do to get to the 10?

If they say 4 or lower:

- That's is low, why so low?
- What do we have to do to get to the 10?

If they don't know how or want to get to the 10, you do not have a prospect, and NOW is the time to move to the next person.

Remember this phrase because it comes into play here. "Some will, some won't, so what, NEXT."

- (Name,) let's review the steps you went through
- Those are the steps you will be doing with your business.
- The first part of the system is simply advertise to find people wanting to have a home based business.
- Some forms of advertising are newspapers, magazines and the internet.
- Do you remember my ad?
- That is one way we advertise.
- I will teach you how to advertise your business the same way that you found me.

* The next step in the system is to call people who responded to your ads.
* You will ask the same questions I asked you.
* This is a mini interview process and you will have a list of questions to follow.
* If you get the feeling that this is something they are wanting, you ask the same question I asked you about their interest on a scale of 1 to 10.
* If they answer with a 5 or higher, you will call me and introduce the person to me.
* I will answer their questions for you.
* That is the way the system works.
* I will help you with your first three sales.
* We will be working closing together until you are comfortable with the business.
* Are you okay with the way our mentoring system operates?
* Do you feel like XYZ and our mentoring system can get you to your goals?
* Why do you say that?
* Is there anything else that you want to discuss or go over with me?
* Perfect, I don't have anything else to share with you.
* We have covered everything you were looking for in a home-based business, right?
* The next step is to get you happily involved as an associate of XYZ and begin your training.
* Congratulations, you are going to love it!

HERE ARE THE SECRETS OF FEARLESS STAGE PRESENTATIONS

You have probably been to many seminars, conferences, workshops and other types of presentations that involved a speaker with an audience. You have heard many excellent speakers, and some speakers who need to improve their message. You have experienced a feeling after the presentation of excitement, energy, being informed and taking action on the offer made from the presentation. You also have experienced the feeling of boredom and being uninterested. What was the difference?

The two biggest reasons for the different outcomes would be the speaker or the material. Most of the time, you know what the material will be before you go to a presentation. Having said that, let's say the difference lies with the presenter.

The speaker or presenter has the responsibility of providing a message that is designed for the audience. The message should be given in a positive, professional, motivating manner that creates urgency to purchase the product or service that was offered during the presentation.

To capture the audience in the palm of your hands, you must do your homework and be prepared prior to the presentation. Here is a list of recommendations for a successful presentation:

Know your audience and be like your audience.

Know why the people are in your audience. An example would be an audience of Internet Marketers who would be interested in learning how to obtain more subscribers. You NOW know what subject to speak about and what areas not to cover. You know their values, pain and desires so you offer a solution to rid them of their pain. You will offer a product that will research and obtain more subscribers or you offer a service that will find the subscribers for the people.

Make a powerful opening line on the subject to get their attention.

Start your presentation by getting the attention of your audience. Using the example of Internet Marketers, say something like this for your opener:

"How many of you need and want more subscribers to add to your name list?"

This is much more powerful and keeps the audience glued to your every word than the typical opening of "Good morning everyone." It grabs the attention of everyone in the room and they want to learn how to get more subscribers. You have the audience in the palm of your hands.

Share information they know they need.

Structure your information to cover the pitfalls and challenges people have in getting and keeping more subscribers to their name list. Let them know it is easier to keep a subscriber than it is to replace or add a subscriber. Grab their attention through emotions and provide the solution with logic. Use data to back up your statistics on obtaining new subscribers and how to keep them for the duration. Show videos of people giving their testimonials for your product or service. Using the third party testimonials gives you more credibility.

Use proper language and speak in a clear and distinct voice. Studies have shown the voice has five times more impact on us than the written word. Record your presentation, review your speech and revise when necessary until you are satisfied with your performance.

Don't be a verbal statue; movement shows enthusiasm.

Studies have discovered that body language is eight times more effective than words. Look at your listeners in the eyes, smile and keep your eyebrows raised most of the time. Use proper posture. Use natural hand gestures. Don't point at the group with your index finger. Dress appropriately, beware of any nervous habits you may have and avoid them.

Close with confidence using emotions and lock in with logic.

The two most important parts of your presentation are the opening and the conclusion. Near the end, you spent all the previous time leading up to this part of your persuasion. This is the time you want the people to take action and purchase your product or service. This is where your energy level should peak and you get the people to purchase your solution. Address the high points of your product and what the product will do for them.

People don't like to make buying decisions because they don't want to make a poor decision. Just use the assumptive close and give them a choice of getting your product. You can say something like this:

"You can take the product home with you today or we can ship it to you. Which one works better for you?"

This allows the people to make a choice of the two options and they did not have to make a decision to purchase the product. Practice this and you will discover that it is much easier than having a person make a decision. In addition, you are using common language and it is easy to remember.

A recommendation on the stage persuasion scenario is to have people video tape your entire session. Practicing your speech with a tape recorder is excellent. Watching yourself on video doing the presentation is earth shattering. The camera hides nothing and you will learn what needs to be improved without anyone telling you what needs to be improved.

THE "THANK YOU" HABIT THAT WILL EXPLODE YOUR BANK ACCOUNT

Thank you. Two small words and yet, they are two of the most important words. When you do something for someone, do you expect to hear "thank you?" When someone does something for you, do you say "thank you?" You should.

This is not hard to learn, it is easy to remember, your credibility will increase and people will remember you when you say "THANK YOU." With all the technology we have today and the time restraints we have, a small thing as saying "thank you" will leave a lasting impression. It is such a simple act of gratitude and appreciation and it builds friendships for life.

In the days before computers, I know some of you can't remember those days, people had to write thank you notes and mail (snail mail) them to show their appreciation for someone. Today we can call someone on our smart phone and say "thank you" or email someone and say "thank you."

Oh, if you are an Internet Marketer with a huge name list and you want to thank everyone on the list for being your subscriber, you don't have to thank everyone individually. We now use a tool called an auto responder and set up the "thank you" message one time and just click it to send to whomever you want. If you are reading between the lines, you know this message is telling you that you can not use the excuse of not having enough time to send a "thank you" to every subscriber.

Selling is about building relationships and keeping relationships. Try this experiment for 90 days. For every new person you meet, talk with on the phone or via the computer, write down their name and address. At the end of each day, write a "thank you" note and send it to every new person. Set a goal for at least 10 new people per day. At the end of 90 days, you will have at least 900 new acquaintances and soon-to-be friends. This process makes the people feel important and appreciated.

Perfect. You now have 900 new friends. But wait, there's more. You will soon realize that your 900 new friends are starting to refer their friends to you for your product or service. These are people you have never met and they are asking you for your "stuff." Please, do not deny them the opportunity to get happily involved with your product or service. After they buy from you, send them a "thank you" note. Yes, this is a rinse and repeat formula.

You are thinking this sounds great but you don't meet 10 new people everyday. This also works for people you already know. To help you use your grey matter, I have listed some mind triggers for you:

Telephone contacts

Whenever you make or receive a phone call, write down their name and address.

In-person contacts

You have the opportunity to meet new people everyday when you are away from home. Start a conversation about anything and make a new friend.

After your presentation or demonstration

When you present to someone or to a crowd, you have a golden opportunity to get names and addresses of you new potential friends. Sending a "thank you" to everyone in your seminar will get most of them attending your next seminar.

After a purchase

Within the note, say something like this: "Thank you for giving me the opportunity to offer my product. I know you will be happy with your investment and I look forward to our future growth."

For a referral

When you treat people in a fair manner, they want their friends to be treated as they were. Share with them that you will take care of their friends in a professional manner as they were.

Anyone who gives you service

Let that person know you appreciate their great service and when they need something from you, tell them to call and you will help them get happily involved with your product or service.

Anniversary thank you

Send another "thank you" to your buyer on the anniversary date of his or her purchase. Tell them thanks for their patronage and you are always improving and enhancing your product or service.

The "thank you" concept is a simple process and too many people are not taking advantage of the power this has for their business. You will make good use of the "thank you," won't you?

THE TOOLS, SKILLS AND RESOURCES YOU NEED—NO MATTER WHAT PRODUCT OR SERVICE YOU WANT TO SELL... GUARANTEED

Within the arena of sales and marketing, there are phrases that are specific to this arena. Every person involved and many not involved within the sales arena, know certain truths about sales. Here is a list of some of the truths. Feel free to add more to the list:

- People buy for their own reasons, not for yours or mine.
- If you don't close sales, you won't make a living as a sales person and you won't eat.
- It doesn't matter what you sell, people buy on emotions.
- To be successful, you must be a product of the product.
- A strong, positive self-assurance is the greatest attribute a salesperson can have.

- The more you believe in yourself, the easier it is to get others to believe in you.
- Different people will buy the same thing for different reasons.
- People always pay more attention to what you are than to what you say.
- It is easier to sell to a person's perceived need than to create need in that person's mind.
- Always present to your prospect's needs and wants, not to yours.
- Handle prospecting as your sales career lifeblood, because it is.
- The better job you do of finding your niche prospects, the better closing ratio you will have.
- The vital part of any sale is seldom the close, but what takes place before the sales interview even begins.
- The best way to serve your own interest is to put the needs, wants and desires of your prospect first.
- To every prospect, any price is too high until he or she understands the value of your product or service.
- To be a value for the prospect, you must first learn what your prospect perceives as value.
- Assure buyers of the wisdom of their choices.
- Let your questions do the selling for you.
- Listen people into buying instead of talking your way out of the sale.
- Your attitude about sales as a profession determines your selling actions.
- Ask your prospects how they *feel* about your solution; don't ask what they think about your solution.
- Listen and focus on what the prospect is saying, not what he or she is going to say or what you are going to say.
- More than 80% of all salespeople talk more than is necessary to secure a sale.
- Associate with positive, successful people and you will be more positive and successful.
- The secret to selling is to be in front of qualified prospects when they are ready to buy, not when you need to make a sale.
- Selling is a science that, when practiced correctly, becomes an art.

* Lack of qualified prospects is the greatest single cause of failure among salespeople. Prospecting is the toughest part of selling.
* Listening is a skill that can be learned and can also be continuously improved, but most of us have never been trained to listen.
* Without trust, you can only sell price. With trust, you can sell value.
* Most buyers are more interested in the person they are buying from than in the thing they are buying.
* Get your prospects to openly share how they feel about what they have seen and heard so you will always know where you stand.
* Enthusiasm grows when you focus on solutions and opportunities instead of problems and circumstances.
* The fatal flaw in selling occurs when you are so focused on what you want to happen that you lose sight of what the prospect wants to happen.

By Bill Brooks

4 POWERFUL SECRETS ABOUT COVERT HYPNOSIS STRATEGIES

You have learned that your closing ratio will increase when you learn and use hypnosis during your persuasions. It will take time and practice to learn your new skills and the rewards are very beneficial.

One of the most common forms of hypnosis is using suggestions. A suggestion is nothing more than a thought or idea that gets accepted by your subconscious mind. The suggestion can come from another person, or it can come by your own suggestion. The suggestion starts as a statement. Once the subconscious mind accepts the statement it then becomes a suggestion.

There are several ways to turn ordinary statements into suggestions that are so powerful the subconscious mind will accept your information. This book has touched on the building blocks of suggestions. You must believe in yourself, gain rapport, use the proper approach and create a trance.

The key vehicle to turn ordinary statements into suggestions is emotion. Emotions are one way the subconscious mind communicates with the conscious mind and another person's subconscious mind. Needless to say, emotions have a great impact on the subconscious mind.

A successful suggestion must have congruency or be in sync with or in agreement with other related information. Whatever you say congruently will have many times greater effect than what you say incongruently. An example would be for you to say, "I'm a super star sales pro" in a timid unsure manner; you lacked effect in your statement.

Let's do an illustration to demonstrate the effects of emotions. For this exercise, turn off your phone, make sure you are alone where no on can hear, see or disturb you. Do not do this exercise while you are driving, flying or operating machinery.

This exercise will demonstrate the power of emotions and show you how to practice autosuggestion effectively. If you have a recorder, record yourself so you can listen to your progress.

Start the exercise by saying out loud: "I am a super salesman."

Say it again but put more emotion into your message: "I am a super salesman." Say it again but use more conviction and emotion: "I am a super salesman." Do it again and say it with even much more conviction: "I am a super salesman." "I am the best at anything I do."

Did you notice the enthusiasm, the excitement, the warmth in your chest and stomach? Did you notice your posture compared to before? Say it again and put in more enthusiasm, excitement and conviction: "I am a super salesman!" "I'm the best!" "I'm persistent!" "When I want something, I go for it!" "I am a super salesman!"

By now your blood is percolating and you are getting into the moment. You did notice your level of excitement increased and you are feeling better about yourself. If you are not standing at this point in time, I want you to NOW stand and say it again with more conviction, emotion and sincerity because you have to believe in you before others will believe in you. Say these words: "I am a super salesman!" "I am the best!" "My thoughts are clear!" "I have a supernatural ability to persuade people to do what I want!" "I reach my goals!" "I am unstoppable!" "I am the best!" "I am a super salesman!"

Keep on with conviction and enthusiasm and say: "I take full responsibility for my life and my actions!" "I control my life because I am the best!"

Now say these words loud enough so your neighbors can hear you and let them know you are a powerhouse. Say these words: "In the face of rejection I always pursue my goals!" "No one can stop me!" "There is no rejection!" "I am the best!" "I am a super salesman!" "I am unstoppable!"

Congratulations! You've done the exercise perfectly! Now is the time to absorb the feelings this exercise brought about and project them in your past as well as your future. Imagine yourself thinking and feeling this way in everything you do and how this will allow you to achieve all that you desire in life! You are unstoppable!

You feel better about yourself NOW, don't you? Did you notice how much **power** emotions hold?

If by chance, any time during the exercise you felt like something isn't right, you didn't want to complete the exercise or you were just going through the motions without giving it your all, it was due to resistance that came from your subconscious mind. Your subconscious mind was protecting you by keeping you in your comfort zone. Even though your subconscious mind has a "safety switch," it is actually holding you back. By going through this exercise you are now conscious of this happening, you have the power to overcome the "safety switch" and unlock all of your hidden potential that was given to you at birth.

You used repetition to create a new procedure. In conjunction to that we learned that suggestions would last forever when we use repetition. The more times you can repeat your suggestions, the better the chance they will stick.

That is why we use the power of three during our persuasions. For example: "By using this cream, your skin will become smoother,

smoother and smoother as you use your amazing cream." We also see repeated TV commercials for products. The repetition causes the suggestion to stick with us for years. For those of use old enough to remember, you will be able to fill in the blanks of these two phrases:

"Pepsi Cola hits the _____!"

"Where's the _____?"

It has been years since either one of the two phrases have been on TV and you were able to fill in the blanks immediately. Awesome, isn't it?

For this reason, I **suggest** you do the exercise we just did every day for the next 21 days. The best time to do the exercise is early in the morning after you wake up because your mind is fresh and the message will last throughout the day. It will only take a couple of minutes and you will notice dramatic effects in the first few days. These are self-affirmations that will help you. When you help yourself you can then help many more people. YES, you are unstoppable!

You just read a form of delivery for suggestions using the **direct suggestion** method. This method works well when your person keeps an open mind and accepts the direct suggestions. It also works will with a group of likeminded people such as a seminar, conference, workshops, etc. Examples of direct suggestions in this scenario are: "Stop!", "Stand!", "Imagine!", "Sit!" and so on.

The delivery method used most in covert hypnosis is the **indirect suggestion.**

To understand what a person is trying to communicate, we have to internally experience what is being said. We need to process what the person is saying, and place our self into his story and experience those feelings. If a person is talking about the great time he had on the cruise and all of the new places he was able to explore, we have to experience the same feelings he is describing. The intensity of those feelings depends on how much emotion he has and the rapport we have with him.

By knowing this information, we can intentionally direct his feelings by describing in detail the feelings we want him to feel. During our persuasion, we will direct his feelings towards our product or service. People have been using this method for years. In fact, great copywriters use this method for sales letters, articles and ads. When you watch a TV commercial about your hobby, you put yourself into that commercial. It is easy to use this method in a conversation.

Use this method in your writings and create your own language patters that are structured to work in your behalf. You can use quotes in language patterns. When you are conversing with someone verbally or in the written format, using quotes allows the receiver to accept the message easier because it did not come from you. Here is an example:

"My friend Mark was telling me the other day that he has an overwhelming urge to buy a new custom-made suit. He wants to get one immediately and he wants to be rational about buying it because he has a closet full of custom-made suits. He is trying to refrain from spending the money on another custom-made suit. This triggers something in Mark's mind and he cannot stop thinking about his new custom-made suit. He begins to see himself in his mind's eye wearing his new suit on stage during one of his seminars. He pictures himself closing his persuasion with the greatest number of sales in his career and he knows that was due to his new custom-made suit. Now all he can think about is that suit and he has the desire and urge to get his suit. He goes to a tailor shop and when he walked through the doors of the shop, he got a rush that goes through his body and he NOW knows he must get his custom-made suit. What is this experience for you?"

Chances are, by reciting this pattern, it will create a feeling of desire for something in the listener. At the end, did you notice you were asked "what is this experience for you?" This is a very powerful way of bringing forth certain feelings because, as you know, everyone is their own best hypnotist. Let them describe their feelings and you just sit back and watch them experience the joys.

Another powerful form of covet hypnosis is **embedded commands.** Since it was already discussed, here is a short recap. Embedded commands are short 2 or 3 words within a sentence that tells someone what to do. When you get to the 2 or 3 words in the sentence, you have to do something to make them stand out from the other words in the sentence.

The last form of covert hypnosis we will cover is **non-verbal commands.** These are very powerful and subtle commands. When you have time, try this exercise. Go to a crowded place, stop and look up into the sky. Keep looking upward for a couple of minutes, and then count the number of people around you looking into the sky. You gave them a command to look up and you did not say a word. When you are in a seminar, church or a group of people sitting and the speaker wants everyone to stand; he will hold his hands outward with his palms up and raise his arms upward. Everybody stands. After a speaker had a good point, the audience will applaud and the speaker will stretch his arms out with his palms facing the audience to stop applauding. If you are walking and you want someone to follow, you will motion to the person to follow you. There are many, many, many more and this is one more:

"You are talking to a group of people about listening. You give instructions on what you want them to do. You say I am going to count to 3 and say now, and then I want you to clap your hands once. Ask the crowd if they understood the message. They will say yes. You begin to count and as you do, you raise both of your hands. As you say "one" move your hands toward each other, then raise them back up for the next number. You then say "two" and move your hands toward each other at the same time and bring them back up for the next step. Now you say "three" and start to bring your hands together for the clap. However, you stop your hands short of the clap. Wait a second and you will hear the sound of hands doing a clap. After everyone has clapped their hands, you say "NOW" and you clap your hands. You just used two forms of delivery for the group to follow. You share with the group that most people don't really listen. The instructions were to clap after you said the word "NOW." We've all heard the saying "actions speak louder than words." Congratulations! You just proved that theory.

This may seem to be new material for you. If it does, you are both correct and wrong. You have been using these words all your life. The twist here is using the words correctly at the proper time and place.

How do you do that? By practice, practice and more practice. You can and will do this because you are "UNSTOPPABLE!"

PROGRAM YOUR MIND TO BECOME A SUPERSTAR: ATTITUDE AND AFFIRMATIONS

You must have a good attitude to do well with persuasion.

Start your day in a positive mood and keep the positive mood throughout the day. Easy to do, right?

If you are thinking NOT then you really need to work on this area.

When you wake up every morning, program your mind for a great day.

Every morning when your eyes open, say out loud, "something good is going to happen to me today." Before you get out of bed, you have programmed your brain for a great day.

Your day is what you make of it.

You can and should do self-hypnosis. Yes, programming your mind is a form of self-hypnosis.

During the day you will probably have to recharge you mind's battery.

To do this, some useful affirmations are listed that you can say to yourself. When you do say these, be forceful and take charge of your destiny.

Only you can control you and only you can be the commander of your mind.

Saying affirmations daily will help your self-esteem, confidence and people will notice a difference in your behavior.

It is all for the better.

Here is a list of a few affirmations and please use others that will work for you.

The list is endless and I am sure I did not put in the best one for you; however, these are not bad.

I do want to give credit where credit is due. This list of affirmations is a list I received from Marshall Sylver. You may thank him for this powerful mind-programming list.

- *I am a powerful human being.*
- *I am strong, confident and have a strong belief in myself.*
- *I know that I can accomplish anything that I set my mind to.*
- *I am ethical and moral in the process of persuading others.*
- *I have a tremendous responsibility to get my product or service into the hands of people that need it.*
- *I know that I am doing something good for my fellow human.*
- *I am driven to help others make the decision that is right for them.*

* I know that other people don't always know what is best for them.
* I persuade with personal integrity at all times.
* I focus on my customer's needs.
* Everything I touch turns into gold.
* I am a people and money magnet.
* I am unstoppable.
* My mind is clearer each and every day.
* I focus on what I am doing right now and it makes me powerful.
* I walk tall, proud and confident.
* My confidence makes me attractive.
* When I look into another person's eyes, I see total acceptance.
* I have tremendous amounts of value to give.
* My ability to persuade someone is almost like magic.
* I know what my customers want.
* I can accomplish anything I set my mind to.
* One of my greatest assets is persistence.
* I constantly close my customers on what I am offering.
* Nothing has any power except the power I give it.
* What I believe is true.
* My mind creates wealth for me.
* I am now taking positive actions to increase the quality of my life.
* In order for things to change, I must change.
* I am power.

- *I am unique.*
- *I am an unstoppable persuader.*
- *I believe in what I sell.*
- *I believe in my product.*
- *I feel good about the incredible job I do.*
- *I know I am not really a salesperson, I am an educator.*
- *I'm helping others get what they want.*
- *Without me, many people would not be as happy.*
- *When I have persuaded someone, I know I have done what is right for them.*
- *I use power persuasion skills daily.*
- *I remember persuasion skills easily.*
- *I persist until I succeed.*
- *I have talents that far exceed the common man or woman.*
- *I respect the common person.*
- *I am now reaching my true potential.*
- *What I think about most comes to pass.*
- *I feel confident in asking for what I want.*
- *Everywhere I look, I find more opportunities.*
- *Money is freedom.*
- *I help others get what they want and my rewards are great.*
- *Money falls from the sky right into my lap.*
- *Other people sense my worth and want to help me make more money.*

- I'm aware that the more money I spread, the more money I receive.
- I am a millionaire many times over.
- The money is just beginning to be deposited into my bank account.
- People sense that I am a winner and they want to do business with me.
- I am bathing in the glory of complete financial freedom.
- Each and every day it gets easier and easier to get all that I want.
- I am free at last to do whatever I want to do.
- I'm enjoying this journey into the adventures of life.
- I am playing my life's game to the fullest.
- Money is good.
- I walk, talk, live and breath a positive sense of well being.
- I am becoming more effective each and every day.
- By spreading kindness I will receive kindness.
- My plan is to add value to everyone I meet.
- I am a positive force in the world.
- The people I need to meet now are coming into my life NOW and bringing me wealth.
- Positive, powerful people are coming to me easily and readily.
- I am a transmitter of potential.
- People are constantly giving me new opportunities.
- Others believe in me.
- I am power.

- *I take positive action NOW.*
- *My life is responding in positive ways.*
- *I am developing my personal power daily.*
- *Life is good.*
- *I feel energy.*
- *I feel power.*
- *Watch me excel.*
- *I am proud of me and exactly who I am.*

For those of you that have never tried affirmations before, I challenge you to apply at least 7 of these each day for 21 consecutive days and let me know what results you have noticed after the 21 days.

For those of you that use affirmations, I commend you and you know that these are super mind programming skills.

Anyone can apply these skills to improve personal success and good for others.

I have given you a list and you choose the ones that work best for you.

THE PRICELESS VALUE OF HYPNOSIS WHEN YOU SPEAK

I want to compliment you for reading this far into the book. That tells me you want to learn while you earn and help people in the process. Congratulations! You qualify and deserve to become $ucce$$ful! It just doesn't get any better than that.

Please keep in mind the following information is derived from practical experience and is no substitute for formal training. If you decide to use the information properly, you will be amazed with the results.

The basic and simplest definition of hypnosis is "the art of suggestion." You see this everyday when you see a commercial on TV. How many times have you purchased the product you saw on a TV commercial? There are programs on TV that use hypnosis as their catalyst to promote products. The one that comes to most minds is a program called QVC. There are many people that are addicted to that program.

Other forms of TV hypnosis are church programs and educational programs that motivate people to achieve their goals. We can go on; however, I'm sure you get the idea.

Of course, the sales pro presents his product using his presentation that programs the customers' subconscious mind into thinking I WANT and NEED that product. The pro used his words to create the image in the customers' minds that they were the ones that thought of becoming happily involved with the product. Perfection plus!

Specific resistance from the customers requires specific words to make the sale. Where does the pro find "those words?" Think back near the beginning of the book. Remember the area that discussed the pros' sales script book? Since the pro did his homework and reviewed the possible resistance for the sale, he had the solution in his mind and was able to verbalize that solution and made the sale. Besides the proper words, the pro did establish rapport, was believable and used charisma.

The pro is a total package. He knows and delivered the two necessary ingredients for hypnosis to work:

* The suggestions must make sense.
* He must create rapport and trust with the customers.

Keep in mind hypnosis can be used for anything and we are only dealing with hypnosis for closing sales. OK, you are thinking what other areas can someone benefit from hypnosis. Here is a short list of other uses:

* Stop smoking
* Weight management
* Education
* Dentistry
* Childbirth
* Stress management
* Surgeries
* Alcohol and drug addition
* Rehabilitation
* Courting
* Building confidence

* Building self-esteem
* Overcoming shyness
* Sports improvement
* Dealing with emotional issues, etc.

Many people believe hypnosis is just a form of positive thinking. Hypnosis is much more than that. Hypnosis is used to bypass critical thinking (your conscious mind or logical thinking side of the brain) using suggestions so positive thinking can be a reality. It modifies the subject's behavior in some desired manner.

A powerful form of hypnosis, which is the one we use and is the purest form of hypnosis, is called "Wakened Hypnosis." The name implies the form and that means your eyes are opened during the entire process.

We fall into a group of experts that use this form of hypnosis. Other professionals using "Wakened Hypnosis" are:

* Advertisers
* Educators
* Motivators

Under hypnosis your customer's conscious mind is greatly reduced and his subconscious mind becomes receptive to suggestions. Even though the customer is in an altered state of consciousness, the experience does not change or block conscious thought. His critical areas, logical side, are subdued and the suggestions are paramount.

The subconscious will accept your suggestions and respond to what you give and create a habit change. Habit change is probably the most important element in hypnosis. Habit change creates behavior change, which creates attitude change.

Changing a habit by hypnosis involves suggestion of the new habit and establishes a higher value of the old habit. This means programming the subconscious mind on the new habit.

We have our customers painting their picture in their mind's eye of performing the new habit and being successful, satisfied and happy. Their old habit will fade away in time from lack of use.

Building positive habits is a very important element in determining your success. You will learn habits can be weights that hold you down or stepping-stones to your success.

Habits are developed over time and awareness of negative thinking can become the catalyst for change.

We go through our day using our habits. Our habits account for about 90% of your daily activities. We start our day by getting clean, brushing our teeth and end the day by going to bed in the same manner as the night before. We get use to our routine. Habits are important tools for our life and they serve as a mean of reducing the demands of our conscious mind for more important functions.

Habits are stored behavior patterns and they fulfill our needs. These habits are learned and that means they can be unlearned.

Since habits are learned, we can change our bad habits by good habits with practice. This is a very important element to remember when dealing with the practical use of hypnosis.

We are concentrating on changing our old habit patterns into an organization of positive behavior and thinking habits. The new habits learned create a stimulus-response sequence for self-improvement. The need for change is desire. This too, can become a habit.

You do have the desire to change for the better, right? You are ready to change your sale presentations to make more sales, correct? You will change your sales routine to incorporate hypnosis, won't you? Did you notice the three questions you were just asked to get a YES response? That is programming your mind to take action.

ACTION or I ACT ON! Today is the beginning of a new YOU! Now that your mind is in a different mindset, go back and read this book again. You will discover gems that you missed the first time you read the book.

If you want to be $ucce$$ful, NOW is the time for change. Step up to the plate and take action. Make things happen for you and your family. You do deserve a better life, don't you?

I wish you nothing more than personal growth and skills and success in your life and I feel like I have helped you in your influence and persuasion.

THERE IS ONE MORE THING BEFORE YOU LEAVE

You know all businesses do not succeed.

Why do some become $ucce$$ful and some fail?

There are many reasons and one of the major reasons for not being $ucce$$ful is explained below.

Please read this closely and do not become a victim of failure.

Many people have **paralysis of the analysis** and never start or take any action.

Others like to get as much information they can about their new business venture and never take action.

Not taking action is a big hurdle for many people not starting their business.

They find many excuses for not taking action NOW and making it happen. Don't you be one of them. You need to take action.

If fact, let's look at the word ACTION.

What does it really spell?

Do you like to play word games?

We will take ACTION and break it into other words. Once again we will see the number three coming into play. There are three words in action and they are "ACT I ON"

If we rearrange these words, they tell us what we need to do to become $ucce$$ful. When they are arranged properly they spell:

I ACT ON

What this word is telling you is that you NOW need to get off of your butt and take action to make things happen. When would NOW be a good time to start?

Some of the biggest reasons a person fails with their business are due to:

* getting around to doing it
* waiting until the time is right
* getting more knowledge
* finding the right people for a team, etc.

What they are really doing is procrastinating.

Procrastination is a big killer for your business.

Most people have never really looked at what this word means.

Let's play that word game again, shall we? You may find yourself in this scenario and if you do, I feel sorry for you.

PROCRASTINATION

We now find other words within that word. The first letters pulled from that word are:

p,i,r,o,n which can be used as an abbreviation for pig-iron.

Let's look at the remaining letters and that will tell the story of why you are not going to succeed.

The remain letters reorganized spell:

DRUM ROLL PLEASE...

CASTRATION

This, my friend, is not only very serious, it can be very painful. It is painful in the obvious way and it can be painful in the monetary way.

If you are in the procrastination mode, you are inducing self-castration to your business and YOUR BUSINESS WILL FALL OFF!

Now you tell me, if your business has fallen off, what good are you to anyone?

If your business has "fallen off," you have no source of income and you will "shrivel up" and die!

You want a list of quality prospects for your business, doesn't it make sense you should be a quality business for your prospects?

I know I shocked you and I did that for a purpose. You need to fish or cut bait.

There are excuses and there are results. If you are sincere, then NOW is the time to take ACTION and make things happen.

I wanted to leave you with an impression of this book and I feel the last portion is something that you will remember and NOW take action.

I also felt this would be more effective than a cliffhanger.

It is now your turn to be like Nike and "JUST DO IT."

THE WRAP UP

Doctors practice medicine.

Lawyers practice law.

Doesn't it make sense that salespeople should practice sales?

Have you ever wanted to take a vacation but wouldn't leave your home until all the traffic lights were green? If you did wait for all the lights to be green, you will still be in your home and never go on your well-deserved vacation. There is an expression that says: "Fall forward fast!" Sure, you are going to make some mistakes. You are human. If you are not making any mistakes, you are not trying.

The only way you are going to get better is by doing. **Review, rehearse and revise.** Live by these three words, here we are with three again, and your rewards will be phenomenal.

If you wait to be good, you'll wait forever. The only way you can be good is to start. When do you start? **NOW!** You have my permission and the freedom to fail occasionally. Do yourself a favor and give yourself permission and the freedom to fail occasionally. Let go of the need to get it right every time and that will free you from your fear of failure. Obstacles, barriers and hurdles along the road are nothing more than stepping-stones to success. You can say it in another way such as: "When you have a setback, you are just preparing yourself for your come-back". By Joel Osteen

A step at a time

The way to influence the future is to do it NOW at the present time. Take mini steps to move forward to your destination. By the yard it's hard, but by the inch it's a cinch! Taking effective mini steps will move you closer to your goals and your success. When you start to use the methods and procedures in this book, take them one step at a time. That will allow you to become proficient using the material and retain the information.

When you finish this book, start using some of the phrases and observe how people respond in a positive manner. At first, your conversation may not go the way you want or you forget how to respond. Don't worry; just let it go. Accept how well the people responded to your words and build from there.

You are in the same arena using the same words. The only difference is the tonality of the words and how you say your words. By rearranging your words, you make them powerful action words.

After you have taken the first steps and experience the positive responses, you feel encouraged to take bigger and bolder steps. You are learning perfectly. Your new feelings of success will continue to feed and nourish your subconscious mind. Your subconscious mind will transfer your data to your conscious mind, which will provide the right words for you to say every time.

With practice you will automatically get better and respond with the right words and right phrases for every situation. You will notice your conversational patterns are getting easier and you are becoming what you are doing.

What you learned in this book is not set in stone. You have the right to vary the phrases and words to fit your scenario. After some time, you will have your own style and personality and be able to adapt to any situation. You have to be like a chameleon and change with the surroundings. Look and listen to the intent behind questions and make them work for you. You are a **solution specialist!**

I want to share the following with you. It came from a Buddhist monk and I happened to discover what he said. His words fit the intent of this book perfectly and here it is:

Watch your thoughts: They become your words.

Watch your words: They become your actions.

Watch your actions: They become your habits.

Watch your habits: They become your character.

Watch your character: It becomes your destiny.

BUT WAIT, THERE'S MORE!

I thank you for taking your time to read this book and I want to give you a FREE bonus gift.

All you have to do to obtain this gift is to type the link below into your web browser.

http://rogerneumann.com/emailm…..inggenius

You may have some questions or comments that you want to share or great suggestions for another product. You may share your thoughts by going to info@rogerneumann.com and leaving a comment on my site.

Thanks,

Roger Neumann

Go out and make it a $ucce$$ful day! :-)

ABOUT THE AUTHOR

Roger Neumann's extensive background in aviation and sales makes a perfect combination for following procedures that are proven to be successful every time. Roger has devised the blueprint for you to have everything you want when you take ACTION.

Learn more at www.RogerNeumann.com.

CPSIA information can be obtained at www.ICGtesting.com
Printed in the USA
LVOW010938190911

246897LV00001B/3/P